Did you hear about the Tronnie who saw a sign saying "Clean Washrooms Ahead" and cleaned forty-nine between Montreal and Toronto? Ha-ha-ha. Or the Newfie who saw a sign saying "Watch For Falling Rock" and carried two pieces of stone into the Nova Scotia Highways Department looking for his time-piece? Ho-ho-ho.

TRONNA ROAST
#1

Don't you mean Toronto ?

No! Definitely not in this case!

With all due **DIS**respect,

It's the TRONNA ROAST...

Ay?

2nd PRINTING — JULY 1991

Newfoundlanders enjoy a good laugh, whether it's on us or otherwise. And, there are those among us who can give as good as we get and better. And, that's what this book is all about.

Why was VELCRO invented?
Tronnies were having trouble with their buttons and zippers.

Tronnie I.Q's match their ages.

TRONNA ROAST #1

by

Rick Trask

a LAFFALONG production ©

Published by
UPALONG ENTERPRISES
Box 429
Port Sydney, Ontario
P0B 1L0

Library of Congress Cataloguing
in Publication Data Pending.

Trask, Rick
Tronna Roast #1

SUMMARY: Presents stories, anecdotes, innuendo about Tronna(T oronto) and its population of contemporary Tronnies (Torontonians), in all areas of endeavour.
1. Put-Downs (Psychology) Satire, wit & humour.

2nd PRINTING — JULY 1991

DEDICATION

To Whom It May Concern

You know who you are... ay?

The Total "Turkey" Population

of Toronto and Ontario, ay?

More Specifically, all of you who have ever

put down a Newfoundlander, ay?

Tronnies...
Running, running everywhere,
To where they do not know.

By the way, it's pronounced New-   -land, ay?
NOT New-fin-lind, ay?
or
New-found-lind, ay?
Understand? It's New-   -land, ay?

a bit o' FUN me son

ACKNOWLEDGEMENTS

I gratefully acknowledge the following for their invaluable contibutions and patience, in the gathering of information and production of this book.

Bob Soper (father-in-law)
Burk's Falls, Ont (Bronson, Fla) - Material

Brad Trask (son) - Port Sydney, Ont - Art Work
Chad Trask (son) - Port Sydney, Ont - Art Work
Jay Trask (son) - Port Sydney, Ont - Material

Sarah Trask (mom) - St. John's, Nfld
For giving me birth in Newfoundland

Maryne Trask (wife) - Port Sydney, Ontario
Patience & Encouragement

Wayne Trask(brother) - Corner Brook, Nfld - Material

...and a note of thanks to all of those fellow Newfoundlanders who gave sound advice and encouragement.

Thank you, one and all.

INGREDIENTS
(the stuffing)

Although lower blows than those delivered herein are deserved, we've opted for the high road approach. Someone's got to show some class in this affair.

INTRODUCTION

Designed to show natives of the big smelly smoke just how much Newfoundlanders appreciate the unique Toronto style and the wonderful sense of humour exhibited in all those "intellectual jokes" they've permitted us to star in, we offer tribute, in kind. It's high time the favour was returned.

Firstly, they deserved a name of similar ilk. These jokers coined the word "Newfie" for easy reference to natives of the greatest rock on earth. So, with all due DISrespect, we think it only fair the world know of whom we speak, without undue complication.

Secondly, we needed a word that was easy to say, preferably with only two syllables. It had to roll off the tongue and be simple enough to remember, easily.

Through 25 years of listening to how the eviscerated ones say the burg's name, we are quite certain none is absolutely sure how it should be pronounced.

Snooty types call it, TOR-ON-TOE. Hurried electronic and print media types say TOR-ON-O or TRON-TOE, while the majority of the working class, the great masses, say TRONN-0 or TRONN-A.

However, for all intents and purposes here, even though TOO-RON-TOO is probably most grammatically correct and TOE-RON-TOE, the most phonetic, we are partial to TRONNA. It contains only two syllables, like gobble, gobble.

So, sit back, relax and chuckle all the way to giddiness, as we pluck the feathers and roast a flock of utility, low-grade turkeys.

Oh! One more thing... while accessing the enlightening contents herein, remember what Confucious always said, "If joke funny when Newfie, same funny when Tronnie. Yes?"

Thanx for everything, Tronna.

Here's a dose of your own medicine.

Here... TAKE THIS!

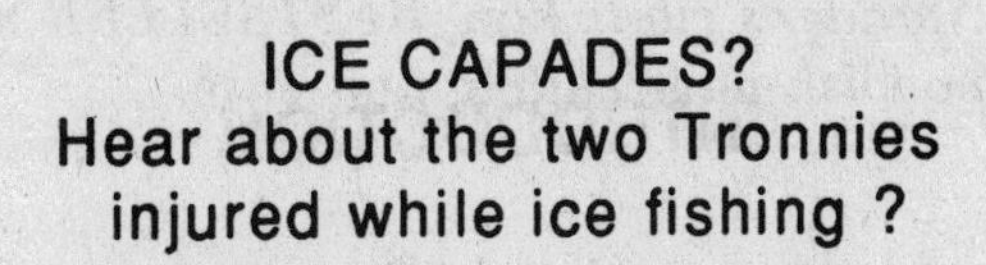

Run over by a ZAMBONI.

NewFUNlander's rib-ticklin' BESTSELLER needles nincompoopish namecalling nonsense.

TRONNA ROAST #1

HEY TORONTO, NOW, IT'S YOUR TURN.

TURKEY TOWN TOWER

Sky Dump

. . .a clever comeuppance

TAKE THAT

A Nflder walked into a Yonge Street haberdashery and asked the two owners, "What do you fellas sell here?"

Realizing the customer's place of origin, one Tronnie winked at the other and decided to have a little fun at the Newf's expense. So, he responded, "We sell a--holes."

"Business must be good," replied the Nflder, "you've only got two left."

PENALTY SHOT

Newf: Only two types come out of Tronna, prostitutes and hockey players.
Big Tronnie: "Hey! My wife is from Toronto!"
Newf: "Really? Which team does she play on?"

GOOD HANDLING

One Nflder asked another what he thought was the best way to teach a girl to swim?
The other responded, "That requires a certain technique.
First, you put you left arm around her waist.
Then, you gently take her left hand and - "
1st Fella: "She's my sister."
2nd: "Oh! Then you just push her off the dock"

A chip on the Tronnie's shoulder is evidence of more wood higher up.

REAL FRIENDLY

How would you get a one-armed Tronnie down from a flagpole? Just wave to him.

SMART 'N SASSY

If female Tronnies were actually as smart as they think they are, why do they wear blouses that button up the back?

UNRULY CUSTOMER

"You'll have to move your feet, sir," said the usher to the Tronnie sprawled across the front row of the O'Keefe centre.

"AAAAGGHHH!" replied the man.

The usher somewhat perturbed went for the manager who immediately took charge and said to the man. "We don't allow people to put their feet up on the stage. Take them down at once or I'll call the police."

"AAAAGGHHH!" replied the man.

The manager returned with the police officer who commanded, "If you don't get your feet down I'm taking you in. Where did you come from anyway?"

With what appeared to be a trojan effort, the man glanced up with a painful expression and said in a choking, forced, almost inaudible whisper, "From the balcony."

MALPRACTICE

About a dozen or so Tronnies sat in the crowded doctor's office for a long time. Most of them were thumbing through a magazine. The average book was about three years old.

A Nflder who was finished and about to depart looked around the room and exclaimed "Believe it or not, those magazines were current editions when I first arrived here."

Tronnie: "Newf, is it true, wild beasts of the jungle will not harm you, if you carry a torch?"
Nflder: "It all depends on how fast you carry it."

SURPRISE SURPRISE
Hear about the Tronnie who bought a used car and found his wife's dress in the back seat.

STRANGE BEDFELLOWS
The satisfied Tronnie business man said to the young lady, "It's a pleasure doing business with you."
Not to be outdone, she responded, "Yeah man, and it's *business doing pleasure* with you."

ECCLESIASTICAL
The Nfld preacher asked the Tronnie, "What parable do you like best?"
Tronnie: "The one about the multitude that loafs and fishes."

THE TERROR
One Tronnie to another,
"Hey, when you get up in the morning, do you feel grouchy?"
"Nah" says the other, "I just let her sleep."

What's the definition of a loser?
A Tronna Maple Leaf fan.

SMOOTH OPERATOR
Doctor: "You have acute appendicitis."
Tronna female: "Listen, I came here to be examined, not admired."

SPECIAL TREATMENT
Tronnie in exclusive Tronna restaurant: "Waiter, there's a fly in my soup."
Nfld waiter: "Sh-sh, be quiet or everybody will want one."

THE THINKER

A little Tronnie boy rushed home from school one day exhausted.

"Hey, mom," he exclaimed, "what a rough day in class, my pocket calculator broke down. I had to think."

NEW EXIT

A Nfld garage owner in the big smoke called up a Tronnie and said, "Your wife just drove in here to have her car repaired and I want ......"

Before he could finish, the husband interrupted, "OK man, just go ahead, fix the car and I'll pay for it."

Nflder: "That 's not why I'm calling.

"Who's gonna pay to fix the hole she made in my garage wall?"

Tronnie: "Hey, Newf," fishin'?"
Nflder: "Nope, drownin' worms!"

Tronna realtor's mind... a vacant lot.

MANHOOD

A concerned mother took her son to a pediatrician because his manhood was not growing like it should. The doctor suggested she feed him a slice of burnt toast every morning.

Next morning, there was a whole loaf of burnt toast on the table when the boy got up.

When he saw it, he protested, "Momma, I can't eat all of these."

She answered, "Just eat one son, the rest is for your father."

TRUST A THIEF

Hear about the thief who broke into a car in Tronna, saw two tickets for a Leafs game on the dash, put two more on top of those and then flew the coop?

PLEASE DON'T BOTHER

The trouble with giving Tronnies advice is... they always wanna repay you.

BUS TRAP

A Tronnie rushed into a hardware store: "Quick! Gimme a mousetrap."

Nflder Clerk: "One minute, sir."

Tronnie: Don't stand there wasting time. I gotta catch a bus."

Newf: "Oh, sorry sir, we don't have a trap that big."

CHRONIC PAIN

Tronnie: "What time is it, Newf?"

Nflder: "I don't know."

Tronnie: "You've got a watch, why won't you tell me the time?"

Nflder: "Well, first of all, if I tell you the time, it'll be no time before I'll be inviting you home and I've got a lovely daughter and the next thing you'll want to do is marry her and I'll be damned if I'll have a son-in -law who can't afford to buy a watch."

FREQUENT TRAVELLER

Stewardess: "Ma'am, would you like a seat by the aisle or the window."

Tronnie Lady: "I better take a seat by the aisle, I just got my hair done."

SOUND ADVICE

Tronnie patient: "Doctor, tell me, am I going to die?"

Nfld Doctor: "Well, let's put it this way, if I were you,

I wouldn't buy any long-play albums."

TACT

Tronnie to Nfld girl "It's because you work with me, that you won't go out with me. We are too close."

She slowly walked to the other side of the room, looked at him for a moment and said, "No. The reason's the same as it always been... you still look ugly from here."

Hear about the Tronnie who didn't stay for the second act of the play because it said on the program: "Act 2, two weeks later."

MOVIE BUFF

Half cut, a Newfie and a Tronnie stumbled into a zoo., by mistake. When they looked around they found themselves standing in front of this humungous lion. Suddenly, the beast let out a ferocious roar.

"Come on, let's get outa here!" said the wide-eyed Tronnie.

"Go ahead, me son," said the Newf, "I think I'll stay for the movie."

A DEER ONE

Hear about the Tronnie who lived so far back in the woods, he had to come out to hunt?

INDIGESTION

The food is so bad in some Tronna restaurants they have to put three shakers on the table.
Salt, Pepper and Alka Seltzer.

COUNT ON ME

Tronna Personnel Director: "For this position, we require someone who is responsible."

Quick Young Nflder: "Then, I'm your man. Everywhere I've worked, whenever something went wrong, I was responsible."

SEE WHAT YOU GET

Three old buddies passed on. One was a Cape Bretoner, the second was a Newfie and the other, a Tronnie. As they passed through the pearly gates an old Pope was there to greet 'em. He asked the Caper if he had ever commited adultery. The man was embarassed, but admitted to a couple of times. The pontiff gave him a compact car to drive around in heaven.

The holy man confronted the Newf with the same question.

In a reluctant manner, he admitted to one occasion when he was unfaithful to his spouse. He was given the keys to a mid-sized auto.

The Tronnie told the saintly one he had never broken his promise and remained true to his betrothed through all his days on earth.

The Pope praised him to high heaven, so to speak, and gave him a super-luxury automobile.

A couple of weeks later the Caper and the Newf were out for a drive together and stopped into restaurant for a bite. There in the parking lot was the Tronnie, crying his eyes out.

They went over to his car and asked what was the matter.

"I just passed my wife," he said, "and she was on roller skates."

What do Japanese auto makers think of Tronna made cars?
Real Remons.

Know how to make a Tronnie crazy?
Nail his boot to the floor and play "Turkey In The Straw"

GOOD TRADE
A Tronnie to his buddy, "I got this beautiful car for my wife."
Other guy: "Where the hell'd you make a deal like that?"

Nflder's advice to Tronnie:
"Don't be so humble, you're not that great."

FATHER KNOWS BEST
One Tronnie kid to another while walking through the red light district.
"Say Mikey. I think the red light means they sell aspirin 'cause when my mom has a headache, my dad comes down here to stand in line."

BULL WORKS EVERYTIME
A Tronnie woman vacationing on the Burin Penninsula last summer saw a young boy coming down the road leading a huge, recalcitrant (hard-to-handle) bull.
"Where are you going with the bull, she inquired.
"To service the cow down the road," said the lad, struggling to contain the beast.
"Couldn't your father do it?" she asked.
"No, ma'am, It's got to be the bull." he assured her.

RIP ROARING EXPERIENCE

The Tronnie went north to work in the bush country. He bought a chain saw. The star salesman from Newfoundland told him he'd be able to cut about 25 cords of wood a day with this beauty.

Next day he returned with the saw and told the salesman there was something wrong with it.

The Newf took it to the back of the shop, tuned it up and gave it back. He told the Tronnie to give it another go, to try his best the next day.

The following morning close to noon, The Big Smoker returned, saw in hand. Said all he could get out of the thing was 12 cords.

Next day, the Newf went into the woods with him. He filled the saw up with gas and pulled the cord. R-r-r-r-r-roar, roar, roar.

"What's that noise?" asked the Tronnie.

DON'T GAMBLE

If a Tronnie tells you he's laying all his cards on the table...count' em.

A VALUABLE LESSON

A travelling salesman from Tronna loved to work in Newfoundland because he always seemed go back home with super bargains he'd find on the island. He'd purchased some valuable old stamps on one trip and 1600's sea-faring documents on another.

During his most recent visit he heard about an unusual parrot. Reputedly, the bird could recant most of the first half of Shakespeare's Macbeth, sing like Maria Callas, the opera queen and recite Longfellow's famous poems. He paid $2,000 for the bird. Figured it was a heck of a deal.

When the feathered wonder arrived in Tronna, not a word was heard from the bird. Nothing could seem to make him talk.

About a month later, the disgusted Tronnie walked into the Gander airport pet shop where he'd bought the creature and asked for his money back.

"Before I sold you polly," said the Newfie, "he could sing like an angel and recite Longfellow. Now, you want me to take him back because you say he won't perform all those wonderful things he did before you bought him. O.K., all right. Because I'm such a fair-minded man, out of the goodness of my heart I'll give you $400 for the bird, not a penny more."

Very annoyed and reluctantly so, the Tronnie agreed.

As the door shut behind him he was sure he heard the parrot tell the proprietor, "Don't forget Willy, my share is $600."

A CHAIN LETTER

Dear Friendly;

This copious letter was initiated with the desire to impart a small measure of joy to all tired business types. Unlike the majority of chains, it does not require you to send money.

Instead, simply send a copy to seven male friends, then bundle up your wife and forward her to the chap whose name tops the list.

When your name surfaces to the number one spot, you will receive 13,371 women. Some should be real winners.

However, it must be stressed that you want to be absolutely sure not to break the chain. Hang in there. Have patience. Believe. One guy broke the chain and got his wife back.

Best Regards.

Your Friend,
Divorce Incorporated.

Tronnies blow their horns the loudest... because they're in the thickest fog.

TALKING TURKEY

If Americans speak English and Quebecers speak French,
what language is spoken by Tronnies?
Gobbledegook.

It is written... the meek shall inherit the earth, but none will be from Tronna.

SORRY ABOUT DELAY

The Nflder waited at the Tronna airport arrival area for about four hours. He finally ran out of patience. So over to the boarding counter he marched and asked for an arrival-update. He was a little worried about his young niece flying in from Stephenville. It was her first flight ever and he was concerned about her being upset by the delay and such.

"What is her age?" the airline rep queried sarcastically.

"She was five and a half when she left," said the Newf.

EGG ON FACE

The Scene is a Tronna Law Office.

Mr. Eggonhisface hired himself a young secretary from Newfoundland. She was pretty, sweet and polite.

One day while taking dictation, she noticed his fly open, so on leaving the room, she said, "Oh, Mr. Eggonyourface, did you know that your barracks door is open?"

He didn't understand the remark, but later happened to glance down and saw his opened zipper.

About an hour later, he thought he'd have a little fun. He called the sweet young thing into his office and asked, "By the way Miss Jones, when you saw my barracks door open this morning, did you see a soldier standing there at attention?"

With a glint in her eye, she countered, "All I saw, Sir, was a disabled veteran sitting on two old duffle bags."

DIVINE RIGHT

In Tronna, just across the street from a church, was situated a topless bar.

One day, a very attractive girl, nude from the waist up, walked into the church.

Immediately, a priest hurried to tell her, "Sorry miss, but you can't come in here like that.."

She insisted, "But, I have a divine right."

"Absolutely, my dear, absolutely correct. And, you have a divine left too, but you still cannot come in here like that."

HEAR NO EVIL

The doctor in Tronna told the spry old Nflder that he'd have to be more careful with the way in which he was treating his body.

"You're going deaf and you've gotta cut out smoking, drinking and playing around with women."

Newf: "What! Just so I can hear a little better?"

LEMONS

Sign outside garage in Tronna...
Lemon-Aid.

WHETHER OR NOT

Tronnie Interviewer: "So you lost your job in St. John's because the weather didn't agree with you.
What did the climate have to do with it?"
Nflder: "I was the weather forecaster."

SMART DOG

Four guys were discussing how smart their dogs were.

Jack was a proud Newfoundlander. Said his dog could do math. Dog's name was T-Square.

He told his pet to get some paper, draw a square, a circle and a triangle. No sweat. The dog did it.

Bill, an Albertan, thought his animal was better. He ordered Slide-Rule to fetch a dozen cookies, bring 'em back and divide 'em into two piles of three each. Amazing. The dog did it.

The Quebecer, Phil, said his pup, named Measure, was much smarter. The dog was ordered to get a litre of milk and pour seventeen grams into a fifty gram glass. No problem. The dog did it.

The three men agreed their dogs were equally smart.

Then, they turned to another man standing nearby and asked, "What can your dog do?"

It happened this fella was a Tronna Union Member. He said his dog was called Coffee Break. He instructed his canine friend, "Show these gentlemen what you can do."

Coffee Break went over and ate the cookies, drank the milk, did his business on the paper, made love to the other three dogs, then, claimed he injured his back while doing so. Next, he filed a grievance report for unsafe working conditions and put in for Workmen's Compensation. Then, he left for home on sick leave.

What's the most confusing day in Tronna?
Father's Day.

AQUANAUT

Girl: "I don't think you will want to marry me. You see, I'm a nymphomaniac.

Tronnie: "Marry me honey and I'll promise you that I won't even take you near the water. I can't swim either."

WHY CALL TORONTONIANS A STUPID NAME LIKE TRONNIES? WHY NOT?

What else are you gonna call people who... act like turkeys, bad-mouth everybody, drink reconstituted sewerage, continue to breath high levels of polluted air, continue wasting lives driving bumper-to-bumper two hours each morning, duplicating with a return trip five days a week for a thousand hours annually, own cerebellums they sit on, listen to the T. Ganges morning show daily and read G. Dungheap's Son column for a daily dose of ugly, allow a senile old curmugeon to continue making a laughing stock out of what used to be one of the planet's premiere hockey teams, allow the Yonge Street Strip thing to continue, believe everything they see on TV emanating from LA and, live in a place called TRONNA?

What else ya gonna call 'em?

SOME THINGS MORE VALUABLE

"What's that awful smelling stuff?" asked the Tronnie, as he peered out over the stage head into the barrel of fermenting fish livers.

"That's blubber" replied the stage owner. "We sell it to a feller in Sin Jawns and he makes Cod Liver Oil out of it."

As the Tronnie was turning away he stumbled and fell head first into the blubber.

After being rescued, he complained, "My new outfit I just bought from Harrison's store, is ruined.

"That's nothin," said the Newf, "now I'm going to have to throw away a perfectly good barrel of blubber."

If you kicked a Tronnie in the heart...
you'd break your foot.

PUT FIRMLY IN PLACE

Two female Tronnies touring Newfoundland in their automobile decided to stop and have a bit of fun with a weathered-looking Newfoundlander who was leaning on a fence by the roadside.

"We're having a problem with our car" they said, "Wonder if you could help us?"

"What seems to be the trouble?" he asked.

"Well if you could give us a bit of carb for our carburetor, we'd be alright."

"I'm afraid I can't help you there" said the old Newf with a glint in his eye, "but if there's something wrong with your tailpipe, that's my specialty."

Ever wonder why Tronnies praise women for their virtue and are disgusted when they try to keep it.

ELECTRIFYING EXPERIENCE

One evening when his charge was high, Micro Farad attempted to promote a cute little spark in an effort to discharge, so he picked up Milli Amp and took her for a little ride on his megacycle. They drove up and down the sine wave, across the wheatstone bridge into a beautiful magnetic field near a flowing current.

Now, Micro Farah was fully aware of Milli Amp's characteristic curves. He soon had her fully excited. He laid her on the ground potential, raised her frequency, lowered her resistance, then inserted his high voltage probe in parallel and began to short circuit her shunt.

Now, they fluxed all night, tried various sockets and connections.

Presently, Micro Farad discharged, draining himself of every available electron. Millie Amp was still in a very high state of excitation and attempted self induction, whereupon she damaged her solonoid.

Reversed polarity and blown fuses concluded the evening.

Hear about the Tronnie who kidnapped a young girl and sent her home with the ransom note?

RIGHT DIRECTION

Tronnie pilot to Gander tower: "I'm about eighty-five miles to the east of you and out of gas. Request instructions."

Tower to pilot: "Repeat after me. Our Father which art in......"

Tronnies are not completely worthless. They can always serve as bad examples.

Keep Tronnie grandma's off the streets. Take 'em to bingo.

A Tronnie's lament: "Of all the things I've lost, I miss my mind the most."

Old Tronna fishermen never die...they just smell that way.

UNDERSTANDABLE

Hear about the Tronnie married couple who finally achieved true sexual compatibility? They have headaches at the same time.

TIT FOR TAT

The Tronnie doctor diplomatically mentioned to his Nfld patient his outstanding bill, remarking, "I don't like to bring this up, but that cheque of yours came back."

"I'm just as sorry as you are, Doc," said the Nfider, "but so did my gout."

SIMPLE QUESTION

The professor at the University of Tronna was not shy about the fact that he was an atheist.

"Unless you forget old-fashioned views and take care of yourself, the world will likely leave you behind," he kept telling his students. "Putting your faith in God may be alright, but you can't stop there."

He continued, "Take rain making, for example. Years ago, when the farmers got down on their knees and prayed for rain, what did they get? They got the dust bowl. That's what they got. Now all they do is send up a plane, drop some chemicals on a cloud, and presto, it rains! No question about that, is there?"

To the learned one's surprise, a young student from Newfoundland exclaimed, "Sure, there's a question... who supplied the cloud?"

SNAIL SPEEDWAY

The scene is the Royal York Hotel, a very special event.

Everything had slowed down to a snail's pace. It was the final contest in a day long series. The snail with the 'S' on his shell was behind the pack. Suddenly, he put on a great burst of speed and excelerated past all the others.

"Fantastic," said one of the snail spectators, "would you look at that *'S' car go!"*

SMART KID

A little boy, newly arrived from Newfoundland, was brought before a Tronnie magistrate. Unfortunately, his mom and dad had separated. The judge was given the unpleasant task of adjudicating the affair.

His Honour asked the lad, "Johnny, do you wanna live with your mommy?"

The lad replied, "No judge, she's beats me."

"How about your daddy?"

"No sir, he beats me, too."

"Well then, who do you wanna live with?"

"The Tronna Maple Leafs."

"Why the Leafs, Johnny?

"Because they don't beat anybody."

QUICK ON THE DRAW

Bushy-tailed Tronnie, rushing into office: "Heard you have an opening for a bright young man?"

Grand Falls businessman: "Yes...and don't slam it on the way out!"

TOOTHY GRIN

Tronnie patient to dentist in Marystown: "Will my false teeth look natural?"

"Madam, I make them so natural, they'll even ache."

Tronnie minds wander..they just go along.

ALIVE & WELL

Scanning the job applications to check for proper completion of forms, the Tronnie personnel director came across one which read: "Age of father, if living - 123. Age of mother, if living - 109."

The director called the Nflder over and asked in surprise, "Your parents aren't that old, are they?"

"No. Certainly not, but they would have been... if living."

SIZE IT UP

Hear about the Tronna midget fortune-teller who escaped from a mental institution. Next day the newspapers read:

SMALL, MEDIUM at LARGE.

TYPICAL TRONNIE COUPLE

She's a rag, a bone and a hank of hair.
He's a brag, a groan and a tank of air.

SLIPPERY CUSTOMER

Hear about the federal politician who moved to Tronna? Needed an election district where the population is dense... from the neck up.

NUMBER ONE MOVES

Hear the big news....

Wayne Gretsky is moving to Tronna.

The great one was ordered by his psychiatrist to move as far away from a professional hockey team, as possible.

EM EYE S S EYE S S EYE PEA PEA EYE

A young Tronna girl applied for a job as a stenographer. She was given a spelling test.

"How do you spell Mississippi?"

She thought hard for a minute and suddenly with a puzzled look, asked, "Is that the state or the river?"

COLLEGE EDUCATION

Tronnie Advertising Manager: "Where did you get this wonderful follow-up system? It would drag money out of anybody."

Nfld Consultant: "I'll say it would. It's compiled from the letters my son wrote me from university."

COUNT ON IT

One day a Nflder received $45.00 too much in his pay cheque, but didn't say a word.

During the next week, the accountant noticed his mistake. Next payday he deducted $45.00 from the Nflder's cheque.

"Excuse me, sir," said the Newf "I'm $45.00 short this week."

"You didn't complain last week." retorted the money counter.

"No,sir," said the Nflder, "I figured I'd overlook one mistake, but if it had happened twice, I definitely intended to say something."

How do you make a Tronnie crazy?
Put it in a round room and tell it to go sit in the corner.

Why don't Tronnies make ice-cubes?
They lost the recipe.

What Tronnies lack in intelligence they make up for in stupidity.

SURPRISE, SURPRISE
Some Tronnies chased a Newf to make stew of him
To do this, they had a great crew of them
They back, later straggled
Bloody, beaten, bedraggled
And said, "It's not fair.
There were two of them."

What's the smallest book in the world?
The Tronnie Book of Knowledge.

Why was the library in Tronna closed?
They lost THE book.

How do they spell losers in Tronna?
L - E - A - F - S.

Why did the Tronnie fall out of the tree?
She was raking leaves.

When Tronnies run away from home, their mothers can't find them.
They don't look.

COMMON AILMENT

"According to your application, you left your last job due to illness, " commented the personnel manager.

"What was the nature of the ailment?"

"Well'" replied the young applicant from Nfld, "the boss just got sick of the way I had been doing things."

FRESH AIR

How do you know your plane's about ready to land in Tronna?

The stewardess tells you to put on your oxygen mask.

Why do Tronna dogs have flat noses?
Chasing parked trucks.

HER HYMN

Heard about the Tronna Sunday School Teacher?
Chased her boyfriend all over the church.
Finally caught him by the organ.

LOCKUP EXPERT

A Tronnie applied for a job as a prison guard in St. John's. Trying to evaluate the applicant's aptitude for the job, the warden queried, "We've got a buncha real tough guys in here, do you think you can handle 'em?"

"No problem, sir," said the Tronnie, "if they don't behave, out they go!"

MOTHERLESS CHILD

A Tronnie lounging around the lobby at the Calgary Inn thought he'd make some time with this rather striking looking chick approaching. He straightens up just as she goes by and gives her his standard, "Hi there beautiful. Wanna get it together?"

She turned with a frigid glance and otherwise ignored him.

Sarcastically, he said, "Pardon me, I thought you were my mother."

"I couldn't be," she shot back, icily, "I'm married."

What's the noisiest thing on the Tronna harbourfront beach?
A Tronnie and a seagull fighting over a dead fish.

NEVER KNOW WHAT YOU'LL LEARN

A Tronnie salesman was checking into a St. John's hotel a while ago. After he made out the registration form, the receptionist asked, "Do you prefer a room with shower or bath?"

Thinking of the potential savings, he asked in turn, "What's the difference?"

"Well," replied the Newf, "with a shower, you've gotta stand up."

SPARKLER

Tronnie: " What makes a man give a woman a diamond ring?"
Newf, with a wink. "The woman."

PROMOTER'S PROMOTER

Picture a new Tronna shopping mall.
Three stores in a row.
One day, the first store owner put up a sign reading,
FIRE SALE.
Not long after, the third owner hung a sign advertising,
BANKRUPTCY SALE.
The man in the middle, newly arrived from Newfoundland, surveyed his neighbours' signs for a while.
A short time later, he came up with one of his own.
It read: *MAIN ENTRANCE.*

ALE LING

Tronnie waiter to visiting Nfld granny:
"And what will you have to drink, ma'am?"
"Ginger ale," said she.
"Pale?" queried he.
"My goodness, no," said she, "just a glass, if you please."

SHOW OFF

Mom and Dad Tronnie gave Johnny a new mountain bike and were watching excitedly as he made circuits around the block.

First time around, he shouted: "Look, Mom, no hands."

Second time, "Look, Mom, no feet."

Third, "Look, Mom, no teeth."

SHORT CIRCUIT

Nflder: "Have you got four-volt, two-watt bulbs?"
Tronna Clerk: "For what?"
Newf: "No, two."
Clerk: "Two what?"
Newf: "Yup."

DUPED

A Tronnie returned to the mall parking lot to find his car damaged. He was somewhat relieved when he found a note under a windshield wiper. It read: "About fifteen people are standing around watching me write this. They think I'm leaving my name, address and phone number. I'm not"

POSSIBLE RESCUE

Nfld waiter in swanky Tronna restaurant: "May I help you with that soup, sir?"

Tronnie: Whaddaya mean, help me? I don't need any help."

Newf: "Sorry, from the sound I thought you might wish to be dragged ashore."

WHAT WIT

Tronnie living in North Bay: "It was so cold here, the candle froze and we couldn't blow it out."

Nflder: "Ha, last winter back home, it was so cold, the words came out of our mouths in chunks of ice. We had to thaw 'em out, so we could see what we said."

CLASS ACT

Number 99, Wayne Gretsky, hockey player extraordinaire, is very popular with kids everywhere.

In Newfoundland, one little fella has learned to count because of the great one.

Proudly, his dad had five year old Mikey count to 100 for his uncle, with no problem.

He began counting and ended with 94, 95, 96 ,97, 98, Gretsky,100.

STEAMED

A Nflder went to a Tronna supermarket to rent a steam cleaner.

When the clerk asked for identification she discovered she didn't have any on her.

"I'm sorry," said the clerk, "we need your driver's license, at least."

"Gee," she exclaimed, "I only want to clean my carpet, not drive it down the highway"

BETTER TRAINING NEEDED

Graduate Tronnie elevator operators are losing their jobs in St. John's.

Can't learn the routes fast enough

TURKEY EGG ON THE FACE

Picture this.

A humungous, brand spankin' new, half-a-billion dollar concrete box with a very expensive retractable roof. Its reason for being? Specifically... to keep out the elements,

the bad weather, so those able to afford the wild price of admission might enjoy watching those at play in complete comfort. Multitudes gathered for the christening. Among them, hundreds of local performers assembled in the centre of the great arena, garbed in a magnificent array of colorful, authentic ethnic costumes. The clothing, in most cases was priceless, if not irreplacable.

The celebration commenced. Top flight musicians played first-class back-up for the swarms of dancers and entertainers. It was truly a magnificent display. A sight to behold. The cavernous playpen resounded in music and merriment. The media was there in great profusion with all it's regalia and electronic trappings. Live television and radio reports went out across the land. Tronna was celebrating the christening of its great domed stadium.

And then it happened as was forecast. The sky fell in. The roof, the half-a-billion dollar roof, was left open. It rained cats and dogs.

2 STRIKES-YOU'RE OUT (AT THE NEW BALL PARK)

Now, the first incident might be forgiveable, you know, first night and all of that. Yes, we, in our great compassion would have voted for forgiveness....if only, it hadn't happened again...like within a day or so?

Yep, jest a couple a rounds ah yer Big Ben later, the blue feathered ones, were showing-off the new covered coliseum to North America via the wide-open window of TV.

The hometowners were doing pretty good. About mid-way through the first inning, one of the birds hit a high fly-ball. Up, up, up it climbed, higher and higher. And then, suddenly, from out of the sky, as the great throng of exuberant fans watched in awe-inspired anticipation....down, down, down poured great volumes of raindrops which just kept falling on their heads. Needless to say, they were not happy campers.

And this, and this, from members of the same flock of eviscerated fowl who would ridicule Newfoundlanders, the nation's intellectual elite.

A wisened Newfoundland grandmother said it right, "My son, don't be too hard on them, they're more to be pitied than blamed."

SLIP SLIDIN' AWAY

Did you hear about the Tronnie Tap Dancer?
Had to give it up. Broke his leg when he fell
in the sink.

REFRESHMENT

A Tronnie got off the plane in Gander. As he was walking down the ramp, he sniffed the air several times.
"What is that strange odour?", he asked
"Don't worry about that, ole man," snapped a Newfoundlander, "that's only fresh air."

RIGHT OF WAY

A Note To Tronna Drivers:
Courtesy is contagious...
start an epidemic

LOOK OUT FOR SAINT

The house looked empty, so the burglar broke in. Suddenly, a voice shattered the silence; "I see you and the saint sees you." it said.

Carefully, as on tippy-toes, the thief took a step to the left, "I see you," the voice repeated, "and the saint sees you."

The burglar beamed his flashlight in the direction of the voice. There he saw a parrot, who said again, "I see you and the saint sees you."

"Dumb bird," muttered the thief with a sigh of relief as he turned on a lamp. That's when he saw the Doberman sitting beside the parrot's perch. The dog was staring with glistening eyes.

"Go get 'em, Saint," squawked the bird, "go get 'em, Saint, go get 'em."

NOT TOO SLOW

A candidate for the Tronna police force, from Newfoundland, was being examined verbally.

"If you were in a patrol car by yourself and were pursued by a desperate gang of criminals in another car doing 80 kms an hour along a lonely road, what would you do?" asked the Sergeant

The newf thought for a moment and then, with a twinkle in his eye, said: "Ninety."

Heard about the little Tronnie ringleader? He was first in the bathtub.

SLEEPY GENIUS

Tronnie wife: "I think I hear burglars, John....Are you awake?"
Newf: "No."

OH THAT COLOGNE

Hear about the new deodorant developed for Tronnies.
It's called "Invisible".
The plan is to put it on and then disappear.
Then, nobody knows where the stink's coming from.

Definition of a Tronnie bachelor: No children to speak of....

WITCH WAY

Nflder to his Tronnie blind date:
"If you hurry you can catch the 8:37 broom home."

BRILLIANT

Hear about the Tronnie who collected burned-out light bulbs for his dark room?

FULL OF IT ANYWAY

Nflder: "How'd you like yer pizza cut, in six or eight pieces?
Tronnie: "Six, please. I don't think I can eat eight."

A STING LIKE A BEE

I was asked...

If I had to, which of God's creatures would I choose to represent a Newfoundlander... which one, judging by day to day conduct and activities, most resembles a Newfoundlander?

My choice? Easy. A Bumble Bee.

A BUMBLE BEE?

Yes, of course.

Bumble Bees are renouned the world over for spreading a very special something through the mysterious magic of pollination. In the process, the bountiful bee is responsible for bringing the gift of life to flowers and plants.

A consistent labourer of worldwide acclaim, the glorious bee produces the sweet elixir of honey for all to savour.

In similar fashion, Newfoundlanders have won a reputation for bringing the gift of light-hearted good humour, a sweet elixir of life and more than just a pinch of pleasure to the lives of other humans with whom they come in contact.

And, you won't find a harder worker, anywhere.

Yessir. Newfies and Bumble Bees are a lot alike.

Another thing worth remembering about the pair... one would be well-advised not to annoy either too much.

On occasion both have been known to inflict an extremely non-pleasant sting or two.

A POEM FOR ME MUDDER

When me prayers were poorly said
Who tucked me in me widdle bed
And spanked me 'til me ass was red?
Me Mudder

Who took me from me cozy cot
And put me on the ice-cold pot
And made me pee if me could not?
Me Mudder

And when the morning light would come
And in me crib me dribble some
Who wiped me tiny widdle bum?
Me Mudder

Who would me hair so gently part
And hug me gently to her heart
And sometimes squeeze me 'til me -art?
Me Mudder

Who looked at me with eyebrows knit
And nearly had a king-size fit
When in me Sundy pants me s--t?
Me Mudder

When at night the bed did squeak
Me raised me head to have a peak
Who yelled at me to go to sleep?
Me Fadder

TWO BY TWO

Smart-mouthed Tronnie visitor to Corner Brook bus driver: "Well, Noah, is your ark full?"

Newf: "No, I'm short one turkey...
Come on in."

BURROWED ALIVE

The Tronnie husband and his Nfld wife were at it again. "Well, why don't you go ahead and call me a jackass? You've hinted at it long enough, he snarled.

"Oh, but that wouldn't be entirely true!" she replied sweetly.

"Oh, yeah. I guess my ears aren't long enough, huh?" he snapped.

"No, your ears are long enough, " she replied, "but you need two more legs and a better voice."

STICKY LIPS

Tronnie: "I wish I had fifty-cents for every girl I've kissed."

Nfld Girl: " What would you do...
buy a pack of gum?"

GET IN GEAR

Nfld Father (calling downstairs): "It's time for you to go home."

Her Tronnie date: "Gosh, but your father's a crank."

Father (overhearing): "Well kid, when you don't have a self-starter, you need a crank."

ONE IN EVERY CROWD

As he was drilling a squad of recruits, the sergeant saw that one of them was marching out of step. The sinner happened to be a Nflder, wouldn't you know? The slick NCO stepped up to the Newf, and asked sarcastically: "Do you know they are all out of step, except you?"

"What?" asked the recruit, innocently.

"I said, they were all out of step, except you," he repeated.

"Well," retorted the Newf, "you tell 'em, Sarge. You're in charge."

SPEED UNKNOWN

Back in the days of the old Newfie Bullet, things were done around railway stations in an easy-going, leisurely fashion.

One day a Tronna businessman, sick and tired waiting for an extremely late scheduled arrival, brusquely stalked up to the ticket agent's face and demanded, "Do you suppose that train will get here before the spring thaw sets in?"

Nonchalantly, the agent casually strolled over to the platform, eased his spectacles a notch higher on an unworried brow, and peered solemnly down the track. "Ought to be here any time now," he said, "here come's the conductor's dog around the bend."

Remember...when you buy a used car in Tronna always make sure you get a full power train warranty and *not just the shaft.*

UNDERSTANDABLE

Two Tronnie gays listening to a husband and wife arguing.

One to the other, "I told you these mixed marriages never turn out well."

OGRABME

A Nfld manufacturer of brassiere's named his product, Embargo. He used the slogan... Every Girl Desires Embargo.

Why did he pick such a strange name for his product?

"At first you might think I was nuts," he said, "however, if you reverse the spelling, you'll see why the name has such great appeal."

FREE ADVICE TO TRONNIES
From Newfoundland Grade Four Students.

A SHORT COURSE IN HUMAN RELATIONS

The six most important words:
"I admit I made a mistake."
The five most important words:
"You did a good job."
The four most important words:
"What is your opinion."
The three most important words:
"If you please."
The two most important words:
"Thank You."
The one most important word: "
"We."
The least important word:
"I"

There's only one thing wrong with being on the wrong side of an argument ...being on the right side with nobody listening.

HEADS UP

Tronna Argo: "I'm a football player and I wanna get my picture made."
Nfld Photographer: "Full face?"
Argo: "No, Half-back."

PIGSKIN MAYHEM

The Argos were having a bad afternoon. Nothing went right. Passes were intercepted, their line backs were failures, and their plays ended up losses.

The captain looked to the coach on the sidelines for help. "What'll we do", he signalled.

The coach immediately signalled back, "Try fumbling."

DUFFERS DELIGHT

1st Nflder: " We were surrounded by natives. They uttered savage cries, danced madly and beat the earth with their clubs."
His buddy: "Sounds like Tronnies playing golf."

AIRHEAD SCRIBES

Tronna newspaper columnists seldom get ulcers. They inflict their agonies on readers.

DOWN HILL TO SEWER
Standard sign on public washroom walls in towns around southern Ontario.

YOUNG LOVE

A Newfoundland teenager moved to The Big Smoke and fell in love with a pretty young local maid. (There are some, ya know.)

Well, as the story goes, he fell head over heels, auctioned off all his treasures and worked at odd jobs to buy her the expensive watch she wanted. His parents were more than upset, but decided not to interfere.

One day, the two lovers went to the jewellery store.

A short time later, he showed up at home with his money still in his pocket. He told his mom, "We got there and she saw a fancy bracelet, a shiny ring and lots of other stuff she thought she wanted more than the watch. So, while she was trying to make up her mind, I got to thinking how you used to ask me what I'd do with something I wanted If I got it. I decided I didn't know what I would do with her anyway, so I walked out and came home.

LUNAR TOON

Two Tronnie astronauts landed on the moon. One decided to go outside to pick rocks while his partner prepared supper.

About an hour later he returned and knocked on the door.

"Who's there?" asked the one inside.

KNOW HOW TO PICK 'EM

Why are there more Nflders in Calgary than Tronnies in Edmonton?

Calgary had first choice.

DIVINE ACCOUNTING

A Nfld priest, a Tronna minister and a Tronna rabbi were discussing the methods, their own in particular, used to determine how to divide money from the collection plate each week, so that the church got what it needed and God his.

The rabbi said he usually drew a line on the floor, then threw the money in the air. The stuff which landed on the right of the line went to the Lord, on the left, to the church.

The minister related how his habit was to draw a circle on the floor, stand outside it and toss the money in the air. That which landed inside went to God, whatever was outside, to the church.

The priest assured the other two his method was best and the fairest to all concerned. He allowed how he threw the money above his head and whatever came down, he kept. Said he was certain God was smart enough to get his while it was up there.

Tronnies take heed...
If you understand everything, you must be misinformed.

NOT QUITE

Tronnie to his new Nfld bride: "With your looks and my brains, just think how great our children will be."

Bride: "And what are we going to do with good looking idiots!"

BRAINY BUNCH

A sign in a brain transplant clinic read:

Quebecer Brains $20.00
Newfie Brains $20.00
Tronnie Brains $500.00

A prospective patient asked the receptionist, "Why are the Tronnie brains so expensive?" The lady replied, "Because they're hardly ever used."

OLDIE BUT GOODIE

Hear about the Tronnie who wouldn't put the right number of candles on her birthday cake because she didn't want a torchlight procession in the neighbourhood.

Why do Tronnies make better astronauts than Nflders?
They have much more space between their ears.

The ambition of many Grade Three students in Nfld.
Graduate, then go to practice psychiatry, in Tronna.

HEAVENS TO MERCATROID (mercury)

Fishing is different in Tronna than in Newfoundland.
Tronnies don't eat the fish.
They use 'em to make thermometers.

FRANTIC FOXES

A Tronnie visiting a Newfoundland fox farm asked,
"How often do you skin the foxes?"
The owner replied, "Only once.
After that the foxes get nervous."

PESKY CIRCLE FLIES

A Tronna cop stopped a speeding car on the 401. When he pulled it over he noticed the Nfld plates. The officer proceeded to give the Newf a hard time, as well as write him a ticket.

The Newf felt like replying in kind, but didn't want the price of his ticket to increase. So, he bit his tongue.

Meanwhile, the Nflder spied a fly circling the officer's head. The gendarme noticed the downhomer staring at his shiny, ever-growing barren skull surface and asked sarcastically, "What the hell do you think you're doing?"

"Excuse me officer, but there's a circle fly buzzing around your head."

"Whaddya mean circle flies? Why d'ya call 'em circle flies?" asked the cop.

"Well sir, back home they continuously fly in circles around horses behinds. So we call 'em circle flies."

"Are you trying to imply that I'm a horse's a--?" asked the cop.

"No sir, no sir. I have too much respect for the law to say that. I would never say such a thing... but you can't fool those circle flies."

MATH GENIUS

A Nflder asked a Tronnie, "If I can guess how many fish you have in that bag, will you give me one?"

"If you can guess how many fish I have in this bag, I'll give you both of them!" said the big smoker.

YOUNG TUTOR

A Tronnie priest was travelling around Placentia Bay when his car broke down and he had to take lodging at a nearby house. He was informed that the only bed space available was with their four year old boy.

During the night , the little boy jumped up and knelt by the side of the bed.

The priest, wishing to show good example, jumped up and knelt by the other side of the bed.

"What are you doing, Father?" asked the boy.

"The same as you're doing my child," said the priest.

"O-o-oh, you're in a lot of trouble, " said the lad, "the pottie's on this side of the bed."

Hear about the Tronnie socialite they called EASTER EGG? Painted on the outside and hard boiled on the inside.

Heard about the Tronnie who looked up his family tree and found three dogs doing their business on it?

DUMB
What's the definition of stupidity?
Trying to teach a Tronnie diplomacy.

GOOD QUESTIONS
What's a Tronnie know about good manners?
What would you pay for the Leafs?
What is the plural of zero times two?

What's the definition of worthless?
A Tronna Maple Leaf.

Most Tronnies have wall-to-wall carpeting, wall-to-wall windows and back to the wall financing.

DUMB OR WHAT?
After half a century they still call their ill-fated hockey team, Tronna Maple Leafs.
Nfldr's learn from an early age, the plural of LEAF is LEAVES.

HEREDITARY
Why do Tronnies act like asses?
If you were half turkey and half donkey, how would you act?

What's the definition of mass confusion?
A sky dump full of Tronnies.

MEDIC ALERT

Recovering, after surgery in a St. John's hospital, a Tronnie awoke to find the curtains drawn:

"Doctor, doctor, why are the curtains closed?" the patient screamed!

The doctor responded, "There's a big fire across the street and I didn't want you to think you didn't make it!"

FROM THE MOUTHS OF BABES

A Tronnie priest got off a plane in St. John's and found his way downtown. He saw a little boy standing on a corner, so he asked the youngster where he could find the Catholic church. The boy pointed, "just down and around the corner on Military Road."

The padre explained that he was a Catholic priest and wanted to find God to ask him to come to his mission.

The lad asked, "How do you expect to find God, if you can't even find the church"

IMPOSSIBLE DREAM

Tronnie: "I'd love to meet a girl that doesn't bitch, complain , smoke or drink. And who is inexpensive to keep.

Nfider: "My son, go down to the graveyard and dig one up!"

Heard about the Tronnie baby who was so ugly when she was born, her mother had to breast-feed her with a straw?

To any gathering Nflders bring a lot of class,
Tronnies bring a lot of gas.

TOOTHPASTE
Words of wisdom ... Speaking an insulting, hurtful word about another, is akin to squeezing toothpaste from a tube.
Once it's out, it's tough to get back in.

TO SHINE
The only way Tronnies will ever acquire polish, is by drinking it.

PERFECTION ONLY
Hear about the Tronnie who willed his body to science,
Scientists contested the will.

DESIRE TO EMULATE MEN
Know what female libbers MS., stands for?
MIZsteak, MIZerable and MIZunderstood.

TYPICAL
Hear about the Tronnies who went ice-fishing?
Came back with 30 pounds of ice.

FUGITIVE
Hear about the Tronnie who started out in life as an unwanted child... now he's wanted in nine provinces.

EXPERIENCE WOULD HELP

Two Tronnies went ice-fishing. They were chopping away, endeavouring to cut a hole through the rock-hard ice when suddenly a voice boomed out, "There are no fish here."

Nonchalantly, they picked up their gear and moved about 20 feet away. They began chipping at the ice. A few minutes passed when suddenly, again, they heard the voice,

"There are no fish here."

With nary another thought, they picked up their equipment and moved another 15 feet. As they were about to begin chipping at the smooth surface, the ominous voice boomed in resonant, matter-of-fact tones, "This is the arena manager. There are no fish here."

Overheard on a St. John's golf course...
Newf Pro: "First tee the ball."
Tronnie: "I tee it. What cwub do I use?"

A Tronnie with a chip on his shoulder has no reason for concern. It's only a splinter from the block of wood above.

SOLUTION

If Tronna business CEO's are as smart as they think they are, why do they continue supporting a pathetic NHL team by purchasing block season's tickets? BINGO!

Tronnie brought cosmetics to a make-up exam.

AGED WISDOM

An eldery lady got on an Air Nova flight in Gander.

During the trip to Tronna, the pilot announced that number four engine had stopped, but not to worry.

To reassure the passengers, he said, "We are fortunate to have three Catholic bishops aboard from Tronna, so we're going to be alright."

The old dear exclaimed, "I'd rather have two bishops and four engines."

MANNA FROM HEAVEN

A Tronnie went to the horse races at Woodbine one afternoon. Just before the first event, a priest went out on the track and blessed the creatures. There were ten in all.

The cleric happened to pay a little more attention to the tenth horse than the others.

Noticing this, the Tronnie bet his life savings on that horse.

Near the end of the race, number ten collapsed.

The disappointed Tronnie rushed up to the priest and asked? "Father, father, how come you blessed all the horses and then paid special attention to the last one?"

My son, you obviously don't know the difference between a blessing and the last rights!"

God couldn't be everywhere, so he created Newfoundland mothers.

Tronnies have mighty minds...mighty simple.

Some Tronnie femmes need a plastic surgeon... to have their noses lowered.

Hear about the Tronnie alcoholic who's never been able to join AA? Never been sober long enough to remember the pledge.

CONFUSED KID

A kindly old lady was strolling down the sidewalk in Tronna, one smoggy morning, when she spied little Johnny crying. She walked up to him and asked, "Young man, why are you crying?"

The young Tronnie replied: "My mom and dad are having a fight."

The lady enquired: "Oh, that's too bad. What's your father's name?"

"That's what they're fighting about." the little fella replied.

Whaddya call a Tronnie with two wooden legs?
A waste of lumber.

Isn't it amazing how Tronnies manage to enter rooms voice first?

GRADE TWELVE EXAMINATION FOR ONTARIO

1. What language is spoken by FRENCH Canadians?
2. Give the important characteristics of the ancient Babylonian Empire with particular reference to architecture, literature, law and social conditions OR give the first name of one of the Beatles.
3. What religion is the Pope? Jewish, Hindu, Catholic, Muslim, Anglican or Shindu? (Check one only.)
4. Would you ask William Shakespeare to - build a bridge, fly a plane, sail the ocean or WRITE A PLAY.
5. What is a gold coin made of?
6. Which team does Gretsky play for?
7. What time is it when the big hand is on the ten and the small hand is on the four?
8. Spell:
   Newfoundlanders, highest, intelligence, quotient, Mensa.
9. How many commandments (approx.) was Moses given?
10. What is the plural of Leaf? (As in Tronna Maple Leaves)
11. What are people who live in Canada's far north called -Westerners, Easterners, Southerners or Northerners?
    (Check one only.)
12. England has had six kings named George, the last was called George VI.
    Name the previous five?
13. Who won World War II? Who came second?

14. Where does snow come from - supermarkets, the USA, Eaton's or the sky? (Check only one.)
15. Can you explain Einstein's Theory of Relativity? Yes or No?
16. What is Ontario famous for - name calling, pollution, NHL losers, stupidity or turkeys? (Check only five.)
17. What holiday falls on January 1st - Christmas, Easter, New Year's or Thanksgiving? (Check only one.)
18. The song 'O CANADA' is the national anthem for what country?
19. Explain LeChateliers principal of dynamic equilibrium force OR spell your own name in block letters.
20. What are coat hangers used for?
21. Spell:
    It, is, not, nice, to, put, people, down.
22. How many floors are there in the 55 storey Commerce Court building?
23. True or False? I tell and laugh at tasteless jokes to be one of the crowd because I don't know any better. True or False? (HINT: rhymes with U.)
24. What is the square root of nothing, multiplied by 10?
25. Where is the basement located in a three storey building?
26. Is Harold Ballard really related to Dr. Ballard?
    Is that why he treats people like dogs? Yes or No?
27. Art Eggleton is a distant cousin of Eggs Benedict?
    True or False?

TOUCHE

An elderly Tronnie who was an avid fisherman recently retired to Muskoka, wrote a letter to Simpsons-Sears.

"Please send me one of those gasoline engines on page 208 for my boat. If it's any good, I'll send you a cheque."

Shortly thereafter, he received the following:

"Please send cheque. If it's any good, we'll send the engine."

Hear about the Tronnie who's wife is so ugly, he takes her on business trips so he doesn't have to kiss her good-bye.

COLORFUL

Tronnie Woman: "I wonder will my husband love me when my hair is grey?"

Newf: "Why not, he loved you through three shades already, didn't he?"

PREGNANCY POTENTIAL

Life Insurance agents are asked for all kinds of advice.

One was surprised when a new Tronnie bride asked him if the cost of her birth control pills could be deducted from income tax, as a medical expense.

"No, madam," he replied, "However, if they don't work, you can deduct them next year."

Hear about the Tonnie who won't buy insurance because his dad had a $100,000 policy and it didn't do him any good... he died anyway?

SYMPATHETIC TOLERANCE

A cool Nflder was asked by a bartender in Tronna why he just stood there and took all the abuse the Tronnie dumped on him.

"No problem", he said.
"I just consider the source."

POISONED

Tronnie Woman: "If you were my husband, I'd give you poison."
Nflder: "If I were your husband, I'd take it."

ANOTHER BRILLIANT EXAMPLE

A Tronnie couple adopted a three-month-old Chinese baby.

At the airport, a friend noticed them and stopped to say hello.

Friend: "Are you folks going away?"

Tronnie: "Yes. We just adopted a three-month-old Chinese baby and we're going to China to learn the language."

Why would you want to learn the language?" asked the friend.

"When the baby starts to talk, we want to understand what he's saying."

Tronnies... merely flakes off the upper crust.

ADVICE TO TRONNIES
It is one thing to be stupid.
It is quite another, to open your mouth and prove it.

ECOLOGICAL MESS
Whaddaya call the combination of the Don River, The Humber River, Tom Rivers, the Yonge Street Strip from Bloor south and the Tronna Harbour?
The Tronna Sewer System.

TRAINED TURKEY TOTALLER
One day a Nflder with an alligator on a leash strolled into a downtown Tronna bar, took a seat and asked the bartender, "Do you serve Tronnies here?"
Barkeep: "Sure, we serve everybody."
Newf: "A screwdriver for me and a Tronnie for ma 'gator."

Definition of dope ring?

Eight Tronnies standing in a circle.

SEX MANIAC
Tronnie husband: "After I shave, I feel ten years younger."
Newfie spouse: "Why don't you shave before you go to bed?"

BEER BUDDIES
The Nflder asked the Tronnie why he put empty beer bottles in his fridge?
The Big Smoke native said they were for his friends who didn't drink.

SIMPLE DEDUCTION
Tronnie: "Any idea what we can give my wife for her birthday?"
Nflder: "Does she like you?"
Tronnie: " Of course, she likes me."
Newf: "Then, if she likes you, she'll like anything."

STOP THAT CAR
Tronnie: "Hey, Newf, what should my wife take if she's run down?"
Nflder: "The license number, me son, the license number."

SOME PEST
Tronnie: "Listen Newf. This is the last time I'm asking you for the ten dollars you owe me."
Nflder: "Well, thank God for that."

THE EYES HAVE IT
The scene...a Tronna golf course.

Two Newfoundlanders teeing-off for the first time. The next green was 300 yards away and chuck full of obstacles.

One of the b'ys shut his eyes and took an almighty swing. The ball landed on the green and surprisingly, rolled directly into the cup.

"A hole in one!" his buddy exclaimed,

"I bet I can do it again," said the Newf.

"All right," grunted the other, "You've got a bet, but only on one condition."

"What's the deal?" The EXPERT queried.

"This time you make the shot with your eyes open!"

SIMPLE AS ONE TWO TREE
Tronnie: "Hey, those trees are growing pretty fast.
Nflder: "Well, me son, they don't have anything else to do."

REAL TREAT
Tronnie: "Do you serve crabs here?"
Nflder: "We'll serve anyone. Have a seat."

FLUB A DUB DUMB
Nflder: "Heard you were terribly sick and the doctor couldn't help you?"
Tronnie: "True. He told me to drink a gallon of whiskey after a hot bath."
Newf: "And did you do it?"
"I couldn't finish drinking the hot bath."

What do you call a fly inside
a Tronnie's brain?
A space invader.

LIBBER LUBBER

There's a story going 'round that some women libbers in Tronna are growing a third set of teeth. No problem there. However, if they ever start growing a second tonque, we've got big trouble.

WILY SEA DOG

A Nflder walked into a swanky Tronna restaurant and ordered the Atlantic Salmon Special of the Day. When delivered to the table, it looked very watery.

A few minutes later, the waiter noticed his customer wasn't eating.

He inquired: "Is there something wrong, Sir?"

"No." replied the Newf, "I'm just waiting for the tide to go out."

MISSED A GEAR

Nfld Manager: "What are you doing here? Didn't you get my letter indicating you'd been fired?"
Tronnie: "Yes, but on the envelope it said, "RETURN AFTER 5 DAYS," so here I am."

Tronnies are proof that an empty head and a stuffed shirt can go together.

CEREBRAL EXERCISE

A Tronnie visiting Newfoundland was amazed at his host's knowledge of marine life and his ability to tell the difference between various species of fish.

"What makes you so smart?" he asked the Newfoundland fisherman.

"It's because I eat a very rare and expensive gold fish once a week" the Nfider replied, "this goldfish is really the king of brain food."

"Where can I get one?" queried the Tronnie.

"Give me a hundred dollars and I'll bring you back one," offered the Nflder.

After relieving the mainlander of his money, the rock resident left. He returned a short time later with a sardine which the Tronnie promptly devoured.

"That goldfish tasted just like a sardine," said the Tronnie.

"See," said the Nflder, "You're getting the hang of it already."

Not to speak ill requires simply...silence.

FISHERMEN'S CODE

Early to bed, early to rise.
Fish like hell and make up lies.

REAL STUNKER

Tronna....world's largest source of natural gas.

PARDON?
Nfider: "Why are you carrying only one board at a time, when all the other men carry two?"
Tronnie: "I guess they're just too lazy to make two trips."

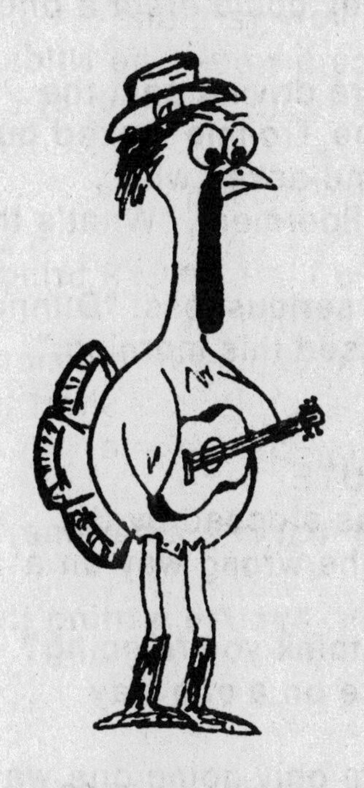

Tronnie:
"Is it a sin for me to play the guitar on Sunday?"

Nfider:
"Me son, the way you play,
it's a sin to play any day."

A SURE SHOT

A Nfld woman was on trial for the murder of her Tronnie husband. Her lawyer was trying to prove she didn't do it.

"Now, my dear, can you remember your husband's last words?"

"Sure," she said, "He was standing in the doorway and he said, "Go ahead and pull the trigger.

You couldn't hit the broad side of a barn."

NOT TO BE OUTDONE

A Tronnie was telling a Nflder about how fast they put up multi-level buildings in the big smoke.

He told him they built the 50 storey Commerce Court in 30 months, the CN Tower in 24 months and the skydome in 32 months. He also told him how they could erect a one family home in a week.

At this point they were driving past the Newfoundland Hotel. The Tronnie looked out the window of the car and asked with eyebrows raised in bewilderment, "What's that place?"

Nflder, glinting in all seriousness: "Dunno, wasn't there when I passed this morning."

WRONG SONG, BUT CUTE

A Nflder, half cut, was stopped by the police in Tronna going the wrong way on a one way street.

Cop: "Where do you think you're going?

Don't you know you're on a one way street?"

Newf: "But officer, I'm only going one way."

Cop: "Didn't you see the arrows back there?"

"Hic-hic. Arrows?

I didn't even see the Indians."

RATED ZERO

Nflder to a Tronnie: "You're number one with me......
and that's as close to nothing as you can get."

A SATISFIED MAN

A Nflder was standing on a manhole cover in Tronna. Every now and then he'd suddenly jump up and down waving his arms and legs. When he came down, he'd yell "86...86...86...86." He did this for 10 to 15 minutes at a time. A crowd gathered round..

One curious Tronnie walked up to the Newf and said "Whaddya doin', pal?

"Ignoring all around him, the Newfie jumped up, came down again and with a large smile, yelled, "86...86...86...86"

Tronnie: "You look like you're really enjoying yourself. Do you mind if I try that?"

The Newfie stepped off the cover and said "No, go right ahead."

The Tronnie placed both feet on the cover and then jumped way up. While he was airbound, the Nflder pulled the cover from its slot and swish went the Tronnie down in the sewer.

Replacing the cover, the Newfie stood on it, jumped up, came down smiling and announced gleefully, "87...87...87...87."

TWO FOR PRICE OF ONE

Two Tronnies were building a house. One of them was throwing away every second nail he picked up.

His buddy asked him what was wrong. He said that every second nail he picked up had the head on the wrong end.

"Well, don't throw them away, we can always use them on the other side of the wall," advised his mate.

BRAINSTORM

Two Tronnies rented a boat and went fishing out on Lake Ontario.

They caught so many, they didn't know what to do with them.

1st Tronnie: "We know where to catch the fish now.

2nd: "Yes, we sure do."

1st: "How will we find this spot again?"

2nd: "Mark an 'X' on the side of the boat."

1st: "But what if we don't get the same boat next time?"

SEX EDUCATION

How's a Tronnie make love?

3 Steps: 1. put-in.
2. take-out.
3. repeat, (if necessary).

SAVVY

The sergeant proceeded to enlighten his men with last minute instructions in the plane before they made their first jump.

He said "When the red light comes on, get ready. When the green light comes on, you jump. When you jump, pull number one cord and if that doesn't work, pull number two cord. There will be a truck waiting for you down below to take you back to the base."

This particular Tronnie got ready and when he saw the green light, jumped and pulled the number one cord. It didn't work. He pulled number two cord and that didn't work. Then he shouted, "And I'll bet that truck won't be there either."

ANNOYED WRONG GUY

Near Tronna lived a farmer named Ralph. Ralph was married to a pretty girl and they had a seventeen year old daughter.

One day Ralph came home from the field and found a note from his wife. She'd run away with a salesman. A religious man, he picked up his Bible and read "The Lord giveth, and the Lord taketh away, and I shall bear the cause."

A week later, he found a note from his only daughter. She'd eloped with a Frenchman. Picking up his Bible, he read again, "The Lord giveth, and the Lord taketh away, and I shall bear the cause."

The next day, he found the house and barn had burned to the ground, and his cattle were lost. He searched and found his Bible in the ruins, he read again, "The Lord giveth, and the Lord taketh away, and I shall bear the cause."

Lesser men might have broken under these trying circumstances. He wasn't about to give up yet, so he went into town and bought a tent and some cooking utensils.

That night, a hail storm came up. It ruined his entire crop, ripped up his tent and damaged all his utensils. Reaching for his Bible he read once again, "The Lord giveth, and the lord taketh away, and I shall bear the cause."

Looking up, he respectfully queried, "Lord, what did I ever do to deserve this?"

A loud voice from above thundered, "Ralph, there's something about you that browns me off."

FORGIVE ME FADDER

A Nflder told a priest he stole a piece of rope.

The padre told him not to worry. It was no big sin.

"It's what's on the end of the rope that worries me, Father."

"What's that, my son?"

"A cow."

DEPARTED & DONE

A Tronnie phoned Air Canada and asked the girl how long it took a jet to go from Tronna to Vancouver?

The girl, very busy at the time, replied, "One second, Sir."

Tronnie: "Thank you."

UNBRIDLED SNOBBERY

Nflder: "Do you like tongues?"
Tronnie: "I can't eat anything that comes from an animal's mouth."
Newf: "Would you like some eggs instead?"

MEASURABLE BRILLIANCE

A Tronnie was trying to figure out how to determine the height of his flagpole. He didn't really know how to go about it.

A new neighbour, just recently arrived from Nfld, suggested he lay the pole on the ground and measure it.

The dismayed Tronnie replied: "I want the height, not the length!"

USING THE AULD SOD

A Newfie was talking to his buddy... every now and then he'd look out the window and yell "the green side up!"

His buddy got a little annoyed with this after a while and asked: "Who are you talking to out there?"

"Nobody important. I've got a dumb Tronnie laying sods for me."

FUN & GAMES

A Tronnie bet a Nflder $50.00 he couldn't drink fifteen beers in a row without stopping.

The Newfie walked outside, came back after ten minutes and said: "The bet's on."

He drank the beers in no time flat. The Tronnie gave him the $50.00 and said: "One thing Newfie, why did you go outside?"

Newfie: "I didn't think I could do it, so I had to go to the tavern next door and try it first.

ONE UPMANSHIP

A Tronnie was bragging to a Nflder about the big restaurant he had in Tronna.

Said he could seat one thousand people easily and had fourteen cooks working around the clock. Said he had a parking lot the size of ten hockey rinks.

While he was talking, they happened to be passing two 10,000 gallon oil tanks by the side of the road.

"What are those?" asked the Tronnie.

Salt and pepper shakers for your restaurant in Tronna." replied the Nflder.

A LITTLE LEERY

Arriving in Deer Lake, late one evening, a Tronnie could find no motel accommodation in the area. He was directed to a private home which offered bed and breakfast.

When told he'd have to sleep with a salesman from Carbonear, he suggested this wouldn't work since he did a lot of kicking and rolling around in bed. He allowed how this activity would keep the other fellow awake.

He was told not to worry.

So, off he went to his shared accommodations. In the morning, he came downstairs looking like he hadn't slept for a month.

A few moments later, the Nflder bounded down the stairs, He looked as fresh as a daisy.

The landlady asked him how he could possibly sleep through all the tossing and turning the Tronnie did.

The Conception Bayman said: "Just before we went to sleep, I bent over and kissed him on the cheek. After that he just sat on the chair watching me all through the night."

NEVER QUITS

The Tronnie boxer wasn't having much luck in the ring.

So, at the end of the 8th round, his manager climbed up to his corner and intoned, "I'm going to hire a detective."

Pugalist: "Why?"

"To locate the fellow you've been trying to find all night."

COMMON SENSE

One of the doctors who worked in an asylum got a flat tire in the parking lot one day. When he took the wheel off, he lost the 5 studs in the mud.

A strolling inmate approached him and suggested he take one stud off each wheel. He convinced the medic the three would secure the wheel well enough, until he got the vehicle to a garage.

The doctor, quite pleased with the suggestion, asked: "That's good thinking on your part young man. Why are you in here?"

"For being crazy, not stupid." said the inmate.

Tronnies are always talking about their inferiors... no one's been able to find them.

NAIVETE OF HIGHEST ORDER

A Tronnie walked into his house unexpectedly one evening and noticed some men's clothing at the foot of the bed. He asked his wife, who was still in bed, where the clothes came from.

She told him the garments were his and she was taking them to the cleaners.

Meanwhile, he went to the closet to hang up his coat. Suddenly, he was confronted by a Newf, bare as the day he came into the world.

Tronnie: "What are you doing here?"

Newfie: "Did you believe what your wife told you?"

Tronnie: "Yes."

Newfie: "Well, I'm waiting for a bus."

SCARY MACHINE

A Nflder who had no faith in computers, wrote down a question and fed it to a machine.

Question: "Where is my father?"

Answer: "Your father is fishing off Cape St. Mary's."

The Newf knew that wasn't right because his father had died ten years before.

He then asked the machine the same question, but phrased it a little differently.

Question: "Where is the husband of my mother?"

Answer: "The husband of your mother has been dead for ten years and your father is fishing off Cape St. Mary's."

BOUNCERS NEMESIS

A Tronna club owner was finding it hard to get good bouncers. Every night one or two of his strong men used to get the tar beat out of them.

One morning he came in with a gorilla on a leash.

Whenever anyone wanted to fight after this, he'd release his new talent to attend to the matter. Usually, it was an easy task for the hairy one.

One evening a Newf walked in and downed a few quick ones.

He got a little glow on and suddenly out of sheer joy gave out with a few bars of "The Squid Jiggin' Ground."

It wasn't long before the club owner had all he could take of this, so he reached down and unhooked the leash. The gorilla grabbed the Newf by the neck and carried him outside.

From inside they heard a noise not unlike that of a three car collision.

About two minutes later, the door swung open. In walked the Newf brushing the dust from his clothes, "Give a fellow a fur coat and he thinks he owns the place." said he.

HUNTERS DILEMMA

Two Tronnies moose hunting in Newfoundland, came upon a set of tracks. After tracking for eight miles, they met a train.

Notice how Tronnies are prone to have a diarrhea of words and a constipation of ideas.

AIRHEAD BARGAIN

"How much are your brains?" a Nflder asked the doctor after he was told his Tronnie wife needed a new one.

The Doctor replied: "Well, we have one here from a university professor. It's valued at one thousand."

Nflder: "That's too steep for me. Do you have any cheaper ones on hand?"

Doctor: "Seven hundred and fifty dollars for this one from China?

Nflder: "Is that the lowest you have?"

Doctor: "No, we have one here for ten dollars. It once belonged to a thirty year old Tronnie, and that's cheap, considering it hasn't been used yet."

BODY OVER MIND

Why are Tronnie women so strong?
If you raised dumbells, you'd be strong, too!

TANGLED LINE

Hear about the Tronnie who went ice fishing?
Brought home ten pounds of ice.

FRIENDLY SKIES

Newfoundlanders complain they find it difficult to soar like eagles
when surrounded by a city full of Tronnies.

If Tronnies had real brains, they'd be dangerous.

TO PET THE TEACH

Teacher's opening remarks to class one morning: "All who think they are stupid, please stand up."

For a moment nobody moved, then one little fellow stood up.

Henry," said the teacher, "Do you think you are stupid?"

"No, miss," replied Henry, "I just felt bad seeing you up there all by yourself!"

GAY TIME

A Tronnie cop walked up to a fellow lying on the street, bleeding and in rough shape.

Cop: "What happened?"

Tronnie: "Will you go up to the third floor and tell that Nflder that fairies don't fly."

SEX TRONNA STYLE

The Tronnie sat up all night when he got married, waiting for his sexual relations.

SPEED DEMON

Did you hear about the Tronnie
who raced in the Indianapolis 500?
He made nine pit stops in all...
three for gas and six to ask for directions.

GOOD POINT

For what reason do Tronnie druggies get together?
A turkey shoot-up.

B.J. THE D.J.

The lady from Newfoundland once worked as a supervisor at a Tronna factory where music was piped in from a local radio station.

In response to numerous complaints from the employees, she called the deejay and requested he give a particular song a rest.

"That is the number one song on the charts this week, " he replied rather indignantly. "Do you realize it's sold over two million records?"

"Yes, I know," snapped the lady, "And I'll bet you've played every one of 'em."

A LADY SCORNED

A Tronnie was walking down the street one day and met a lady of ill-repute. She asked for twenty dollars and he told her he wouldn't go any higher than five.

Two days later, while walking down the same street with his wife, he met the same lady. Suddenly, she recognized him. "See what you get for five bucks," said she, with a satisfied glare.

DON'T KNOCK COMMON SENSE

Nflder: "Why do you keep hitting yourself on the head with a hammer?"

Tronnie: "Because it feels so good when I stop."

DELIGHTFUL

Why is there a cake at a Tronnie wedding?

To keep the flies off the bride.

INTELLECTUALS ON PARADE

The bumper-to-bumper 4-6 pm QEW & 401 traffic through Tronna. The daily grind.

The joke is... these same brainy plebes, prone to ridicule, to slight the intellectual capacity of Nflders at the drop of a hat, are the same turkeys who spend countless hours in cars, time equal to about 50 days over a 12 month period, moving at 10-20 mph for 40-50 miles on super highways.

This strange phenomenon happens twice-a-day, five days a week, all year-round. Little wonder they're mad at the world and bad-mouth everybody.

You'll never guess what they call that time period?

RUSH HOUR.

BATH TIME

How do you get Tronnies out of a pool, fast?

Throw in a bar of soap and fresh water.

SIDEWAYSUPUNDERANDALLAROUND

Nfider: "Why is the nurse chasing that fellow with a kettle of boiling water?"

Doctor: "That stupid woman. I told her to boil the water and sterilize the instruments to prick his boil."

"She gets everything backwards."

BUNNY PUNNY

A Tronnie walked into a restaurant in Corner Brook and asked for half a rabbit.

Waitress: "Sorry, sir, we don't split hares."

LIMITED COMPANY

A Nflder decided to form a dummy corporation.

So, he sent 25 invitations to Tronnies.

BROTHERLY LOVE

A Tronnie was overseas for three years when he received a letter from his wife. It contained news of his recent change of status. He had become the father of a nine-pound baby boy.

Tronnie went to the canteen, bought a box of cigars, and passed them around.

Taking a cigar, the Corporal asked, "How can you be the father Tronnie? You've been over here for three years."

Tronnie: "So what? There's three years between me and my brother."

PARDON THE PARSON

This Nflder in Tronna didn't have much liking for Tronnies.

He was driving down the street one day, saw one riding a bike on the side of the road. Bumped him with his car.

The Tronnie went away limping and bleeding. The Nflder drove away laughing.

After driving a ways, he picked up a priest with a briefcase.

A little further down the road he saw another Tronnie. He didn't think it would be right to hit this fellow with the priest in the car, so he decided to get close to him and just give him a little scare.

He speeded up a bit and as he passed the guy, he heard a loud thud.

Startled, he asked, "What was that?"

"You looked like you were gonna miss him, so I wacked him with my briefcase." said the padre.

RESPECT

Bell Boy: "Can I carry your bag, Sir?"
Tronnie: "Nah, let her walk."

NFLD WIT

A Tronnie tourist in Nfld asked his guide:
"Guess you've lived here all your life?"
Nflder replied: "No, not yet.

Hear about the Tronnie who dreamt he died?
The heat woke him up.

MAKES SENSE

A Tronnie followed a Nflder all the way down the TCH to North Sydney.

He thought it seemed strange that just before the Newf got to weigh scales he'd get out, throw rocks at his truck, walk around and kick it on both sides.

At North Sydney he approached the Newf and asked why he did what he did to the truck on the way down.

The Nflder explained, "As you can see I have a half ton truck. I am carrying one ton of budgie birds to Newfoundland. So, if I don't keep half of them little fellows flying when I hit the weight scales, I'll be overweight.

DO IT EVERYTIME

Tronnie on his way to Newfoundland saw a sign saying...

CLEAN WASHROOMS AHEAD.

So, he cleaned every public washroom on the way down.

INTELLECTUALISM

1st Tronnie: "If I can guess how many fish you have in that bag, will you give me one?"

2nd Tronnie: "If you can guess how many fish I have in this bag, I'll give you both of them."

Tronnie: "It must be very difficult for a man with a mustache to eat soup?"
Nflder: "Yes sir, quite a strain."

WASTE NOT
Why do seagulls from Newfoundland fly upside-down over Tronna?

Nothing down there worth doing droppings on.

DELIGHTFUL
Hear about the new eau-de-cologne developed especially for Tronnies?
It's got a fowl aroma.

PIED PEEPER
Heard about the guy who was going out with a Tronnie girl who was so ugly that a peeping Tom reached in and pull down the shades?

TRONNIE BRIGHT BOY

Tronnie's buddy was telling him how to go about getting a job in the mine.

"First," he said, "He will ask you if you ever worked in a mine before. Tell him yes.

Second, he will ask how deep you've worked. Tell him one or two thousand feet.

Then, he will ask you a few simple questions." his friend continued.

"To tell you the truth, anybody can get a job here." he added.

Tronnie went inside and the manager asked: "Have you ever

worked in a mine before?"

Tronnie: "Yes Sir, for years and years."

Manager: "Good. How deep did you work?"

Tronnie: "Three thousand feet."

Manager: "Very good. That's the kind of men we want here.

Tell me. What type of light did you use on your hat?"

Tronnie: "No lights, sir. You see, I worked all day shifts."

Hear about the Tronnie claims he dines with the brass? Wouldn't trust him with the silver.

SEEING IS BELIEVING

Four Tronnies attacked a Nflder in Tronna. The Newf said they battled for half an hour and he managed to keep them away.
He said he would never have managed it, if it weren't for his white cane.

FACT STRANGER THAN FICTION
Two reasons why The Lord wasn't born in Tronna?
Neither three wise men nor a virgin could be found.

A BEAUT
Hear about the beauty contest staged in Tronna?
Nobody won.

WATER ON BRAIN
Have ya heard about the Tronnie fisherman who wanted to be buried in Lake Ontario?
Two sons drowned while digging his grave.

SKI NUT
A Newf gifted a Tronnie with a pair of water-skiis for his birthday.
Tronnie spent all summer looking for a hill with running water.

PRETTY FAST
A Tronnie ran into his house one day, all out of breath, and said; "I ran all the way from work behind a bus and saved a dollar."
Wife: "Why didn't you run home behind a taxi and save fifteen."

How do Tronnies say, "To Hell With You?"
Trust Me.

TOUGH TRONNIE

A Tronnie fought with a Nflder for fifteen minutes before throwing him over the stairs. Then, he threw the Newf's wheelchair down after him.

NFLD ENTREPRENEURISM

$200,000 dollars is too steep for me." the Nflder told the Tronnie realtor, "Do you have anything cheaper?"

Salesman: "I have one home listed for $98,000."

"Still too high. Is that all you have?" asked the Newf.

By this time the salesman was getting more than a little annoyed with this guy. So, just for the heck of it, he said, "Yes, it just happens we have an out-house going for five hundred."

The astonished saleman couldn't believe his ears when he heard the Newf say, "I'll take it,"

About a month later, purely by accident, the salesman met the Nflder on the street. They exchanged pleasantries and then the realtor asked, "How are you making out in your new home?"

"Oh, just great, the Newf responded, I'm also earning a little extra money with it."

"Is that so? How?" he asked somewhat bemusedly.

"I rented the basement apartment to a Tronnie." glinted the one-upman.

Tronnies light up rooms by leaving.

MAMA'S BOY
Why do Tronnie men have mustaches?
So they can look like their mothers.

MAKING MOUTHPIECES
Why do grown-up Tronnies who should know better, continue bad-mouthing everybody?
Can't help it. It's hereditary. Parents bred 'em that way.

CARE LESS
Why do scientists breed Tronnies instead of rats for experiments?
They multiply faster and nobody gets attached to them.

BINGO
Why isn't there a market for Preparation 'H' in Tronna?
'cause when God created Tronnies, he made perfect a--holes.

SERVICE WITH SMILE
Why do Nflder's in Tronna throw away their garbage in clear plastic bags?
So Tronnies can go window shopping.

B.S.
What's wrong with the Tronnie with the brown ring around his neck?
Down a quart.

TRONNA MAPLE LEAVES HOCKEY SCHEDULE

Jan.	11	Muskoka Jr. High
	17	North Bay Cub Scout Troop 101
	26	Ontario Blind Academy
Feb.	03	Spanish American War Vets
	10	Tronna Crippled Children's Hospital
	17	St. Cloud Home for Wayward Girls
	24	Kitchener Girl Guides Troop 69
Mar.	01	Sarnia VD Clinic Post
	07	Etobicoke Boys Choir
	12	Korean War Amps
	21	VA Hospital Polio Patients

SPECIAL MONDAY NIGHT GAME

Mar. 08 .... Utopia Gay Boys

RULE CHANGES FROM LAST YEAR

1. When playing polio patients, Leaves must not disconnect leg braces.
2. When playing the Girl Scouts, Leaves must not hide their cookies.
3. When playing the blind academy, Leaves must not hide the puck.
4. When playing the Korean War Amps,Leaves must not file any protest against players with one leg indicating they are harder to body check.

LEAVES SCHEDULE
(continued)

RULES REMAINING SAME AS LAST YEAR

1. A goal is still worth 5 points. (For all you Leaf fans who've never seen one. This phenomenon occurs when the puck is shot over the goal line.)
2. The Leaves will be allowed 12 men on the ice at all times.
3. The Leaves will be allowed 20 time-outs, as opposed to 3 for the other team.
4. The Leaves will be allowed to substitute kindergarten hockey champs at any time during the course of the game.
5. The Leaves will be awarded a penalty shot each time they cross the other teams blue line.

NAME CHANGE

The Tronna Maple Leafs name will be changed to the Tronna Tampons, since they're good for only one period and don't have a second string.

COACHING CHANGES

Coach Carpenter is expected to be hammered and nailed to the wall. He'll be replaced by Coach Plumber, the drain brain.
It'll make more sense since eveything's been going down the tubes lately, anyway.

BRAIN CHILD
Hear about the Tronnie who froze to death at a Drive-In?
She was waiting to see CLOSED FOR THE SEASON.

LOBOTOMY SPECIAL
Hear about the Tronnie who had a neurological operation?
She had a brain installed.

IT WORKS
What do they call the combination of the Humber River, the Don River, Tom Rivers, the Yonge Street Strip and Tronna Harbour?
The Tronna Sewer System.

ENOUGH OF THAT GARBAGE
Lately, Tronnies have been having trouble finding appropriate dumping locations for refuse, in surrounding municipalities and elsewhere.
Judging by the filth that comes out of their mouths, they must be eating a lot of it,

Tronnies favourite party-pack is a case of verbal diarrhea.

UPSIDEDOWN
Why do Tronnies have sore brains?
'cause they sit on 'em.

HOT TIP

The scene is the Deer Lake airport.

Passengers just completed boarding an AIR NOVA flight, bound for Tronna.

Two natives of The Big Smoke, both considering a move to the island, became involved in conversation. The topic concerned prospective towns to which they might move.

"I don't think I wanna live in Badger," said one, "services are questionable and no Tronnies there."

"Bay Roberts doesn't appeal to me for the same reason," said the other, "none of us there, either."

Overhearing the two, an older lady from the seat behind, felt compelled to suggest, "Why don't you book a flight to hell, you'll feel right at home down there."

UNBELIEVABLE

Then there was the little Tronna boy who was so shy, his mother had to blindfold his rubber duck to get him in the tub.

Hear about the Tronnie who said she was eighteen and her husband thirty when they met? Now he's sixty, so she figures since he's twice as old as he was then, she must be 36.

BASIC MATH

Hear about the Tronna Rubix cube?
It's white on all sides
and takes a Tronnie two minutes to solve.

OBVIOUS OBSERVATION

What do people say when they see a group of Tronnies together?
"Whadda buncha turkeys."

POWERFUL PAIN

Word is... the population at Kingston Penitentiary will riot next time they are forced to watch THE KNASHTIONAL with Knowlton Knash.
Inmates claim cruel & unbearable punishment in the first degree.

A BETTER IDEA

How do Tronnies install light bulbs?
One holds the bulb while the other five turn the chair.

GOOD THINKING

Nflder: "What was the big explosion on your buddy's farm?"
Tronnie: "He fed his chickens some lay-or-bust feed.
One of them was a rooster."

UNSELFISH

The Nflder to his new Tronnie girlfriend: "Now, let's talk about you, shall we?"
"All right, dear." answered she.
"Well then, now tell me, *what does a girl like you* see in a boy like me?"

DEATH WARMED OVER

A Nfld mortician was discussing business with a Tronnie associate over coffee one day.

"I love my advertising business because I can create new ideas, new campaigns, new slogans for my clientele. It's exciting. They appreciate me for that." said the ad exec.

"What have you come up with lately? asked the Nflder.

"A beauty" said the beaming Tronnie. "Just coined a slogan for a client who sells highway signs. Because his advertising sits there for so long it, REMAINS TO BE SEEN."

"Mind if I use it too? asked the Newf, "I've got lots of remains to be seen."

INDOCTRINATION

Why are Tronnie kids like they are?
If you were exposed to extremely high levels of stupidity, like they've been,
you wouldn't be too bright yourself.

Hear about the Tronnie who
applied for a job at the Oshawa GM plant.
Studied 10 days for a urine test.

PROPER DIRECTION

Why is Tronna City Hall shaped like only half a circle?
The engineers lost the architect's blueprints.

A DOG CALLED SEX

It seems everybody who gets a dog calls him either Rover or Boy. To be different, I called mine Sex. To my surprise, it wasn't long before I found this to be an embarassing name.

One day, I took Sex for a walk and he ran away from me. I spent hours looking for him. A cop approached me and asked, " What are doing. in this alley at four in the morning?" I said, "I'm looking for Sex." My case comes up next Thursday.

I went to City Hall to get him a licence. I told the clerk, "I would like to have a licence for Sex." He said, "I would like to have one, too!" Then I said, "But, this is a dog!". He said he didn't care how she looked. Then I said, "You don't understand. I've had Sex since I was two years old." He replied, "You must have been a very strong baby!"

My wife and I separated and we went to court to fight for custody of the dog. I said,"Your Honour, I had Sex before we were married." The Judge said, "Me too!" I went on to explain how I had sex on TV. He called me a show-off. When I told him it was a contest, he asked me if I sold tickets.

I tried to explain about the time my wife and I were on our honeymoon and we took the dog. When I checked into the motel I told the clerk I wanted a room for my wife and me, and a special room for Sex. He told me that every room was for Sex. I said, "You don't understand. Sex keeps me awake at night." The clerk said, "Me too."

I gave up.

My next dog will be named Rover or Boy, anything but SEX.

Tronnie: "Newf, is it true, wild beasts of the jungle will not harm you, if you carry a torch?"
Nflder: "It all depends on how fast you carry it."

SALUTE

And then there was the Tronnie who was voted "Man of the Hour?" You gotta watch him every minute.

Tronnie minds... all at the tip of their tongues.

Hear about the Tronnie who never drinks more than he can stand?
The minute he can stand, he starts drinking again.

JEALOUSY

Why are Tronnies jealous of Nflders?
'Cause Nflders have deep-rooted pride.
Tronnies exhibit deep-ruded snide.

WITHOUT PREJUDICE

Tronnies call us names, like goofy Newfies. Others they call Niggers, Kikes, Dagos, Grease-balls, Spicks, Slants, Jungle Bunnies, Frogs and many more, too disgusting to print. However, we gotta say one thing in their defense.
They're not prejudiced.
They hate everybody.

CHILDISH ADVICE

There are about three million Tronnies breathing in the big smoke. Judging by the way they do what they do, it is evident The Lord has not been kind to them.

It becomes more and more apparent as time goes by that brainpower is in extremely short supply, amongst the flock. It is such that a team of Lobotomy Specialists could thrive in the midst of the deficient throng.

In lieu of that kind of unlikely major medical undertaking, a humanitarian gesture of the highest order has been put forth.

It's not a lot, but it's a start.

A class of Grade Five students from Krinkle Cove, Newfoundland, recognizing the plight of some poor dumb fowl, offers the following tip, gratis.

If any Tronnie happens upon this roasting, accidentally or otherwise, the kids suggest they trot this advice to the turkeys on the round table, toute suite, if not sooner.

THE TIP... It's not smart to dump sewerage and other junk in your harbour and then expect to swim in it.

Hear about the Tronnie psychiatrist?
Always trying to get a girl on the couch.

EARLY RISER

Hear about the Tronnie who is so dumb...
she thinks Kamloops is a breakfast cereal.

A DEAR PRICE TO PAY

A Newfoundlander who spent a long time in Tronna decided one day he'd had enough, so he planned a move back to St.John's.

He was home about a week when one evening he felt like having the company of a young woman.

He knew right where to go. The house was exactly where he was told it would be, you know, one of ill-repute. He went inside and asked for Maybel. Half an hour later, after finishing his business dealings, he asked her about the charge. "Seventy-five dollars ," said the young thing. So he took out his money and peeled off two hundred. "That's too much, sir," said she.

"Keep it, my dear, it was worth it."

About a week later, he was feeling that way again. So, off he went to enjoy Mabel's delights. After it was over, she again requested seventy-five. He handed her two hundred. She again indicated the overpayment. He responded the way he did on the previous occasion. Said it was indeed worth it.

Another week passed. He decided it was time again. Following completion of the transaction, she said, "Seventy-five, as usual." He handed her two hundred. She then queried, "By the way, where are you from?

"Tronna." said he. "That's funny, so am I." said she.

"I know." said he, "Your father asked me to bring you down six hundred dollars."

ADVICE TO TRONNIES
It is far better to remain silent on subjects of which you know nothing than to speak and remove all doubt.

What's got a pea-sized brain, bad-mouths everybody and looks like a turkey?
A Tronnie.

Hear about the Tronnie called QUITS?
After his birth his parents decided to call it quits.

It's not that Tronnies don't have presence of mind...its just the absence of thought.

DO TELL
Heard the walls in Tronna apartment buildings are so thin, when a person peels onions in one, the next door neighbours start to cry.

PETRO FOWL
Environment officials noticed two oil slicks on Lake Ontario during a routine aerial check. Upon closer examination, they found it was only two Tronnies swimming to shore.

Tronnies...soft hearts and heads to match.

T.O.
Back in the sixties when Tronnie yuppies were mere puppies, they had difficulty pronouncing the name of their hometown. (too many syllables.) They called it T. O. (was that short for... Toilet, Ontario?)

COUSINS?
You know what really bothers Tronnies?
What really gets to them?
AMERICANS. Yes. Cousins to the south.
Great turkey roasters.
They keep 'em hot.
Yanks always refer to Tronna as "Where?"
And Tronnies as, "Who?"
The truth is... most Americans really don't know Tronna exists and could care less.
This irritates Tronnies no end. This really rots their socks. They think their long concrete tower and new ball park should get them more respect from the cousins to the south. No chance.
One thing ya gotta admire about Yanks... dey knows turkeys when dey sees 'em.

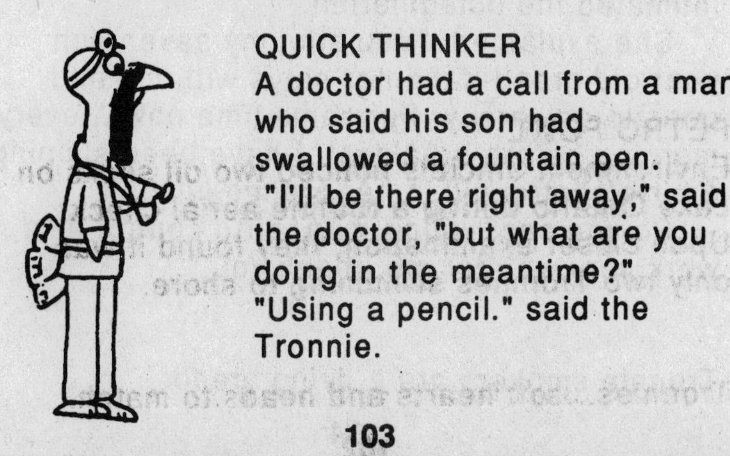

QUICK THINKER
A doctor had a call from a man who said his son had swallowed a fountain pen.
"I'll be there right away," said the doctor, "but what are you doing in the meantime?"
"Using a pencil." said the Tronnie.

FALSE BOTTOM

Guess what they're putting on the bottom of beer bottles, next month, in Tronna? Open other end.

GREAT GRANNY PILLS

An eighty year old Newfoundland lady asked her doctor for some birth control pills.

The physician told her she didn't need that kind of medication at her grand age. She insisted. He asked why she was being so stubborn.

She responded, "Because the birth control pills are like sleeping pills to me.

Puzzled, the doctor explained, "Ma'am, with all due respect, I know what's in birth control pills and I know what's in sleeping pills. I can assure you, there's nothing in birth control pills that will make you sleep."

"With all due respect to you young man, you're wrong," she said with a grin. "the birth control pills I've been using, have worked extremely well. I have had many, many sound nights of sleep, thanks to those little darlings," intimated the octaginarian.

She explained, "You see, my seventeen year old grand-daughter stays with me and goes to university. For some time now... every morning before breakfast, I have been slipping a birth control pill in her orange juice.

So you see, young man, birth control pills work very well for me, thank you."

Tronnie smokers are a dying breed.

ABOVE IT ALL

Nflder : "Suppose you've heard the joke about the roof?"
Tronnie: "Don't think so."
Nflder: "Oh well. Don't worry 'bout it. It's over your head anyway."

YOU BE THE JUDGE

Hear about the gay Tronnie magistrates? Tried each other.

SWEET SUCCESS

Success is not measured by other people's standards.
Success is measured by how you use what you've got.

BRIGHT BOY

The Nflder asked the Tronnie if he'd heard about another Tronnie who stayed awake all night trying to figure out where the sun went, when it went down?
Tronnie: "No. What happened?"
Newf: "It finally dawned on him."

Newf: "Did I see you pushing your bicycle to work yesterday."
Tronnie: "Yes. I was so late, I didn't have time to get on."

You never fail...until you stop trying.

NAUGHTY BIRD

A snooty Tronnie woman from a well-too-do neighbourhood wanted a parrot for a pet. She inquired all over town, only to discover they were in very short supply.

However, she did get word on one which lived close to her. It was owned by a lady who ran a house of ill-repute and the bird had a major defect which, she was warned might prove to be embarrasing on any given occasion. The bird swore like a trooper. He'd come out with a mouthful without warning.

The uppidy suburbanite wanted a parrot so bad, she decided it didn't matter from where it came or what it's language. She wanted a parrot, period. She'd take the chance. So, she talked to the owner and made arrangements to buy the bird.

Well, lo and behold, as luck would have it, the first night she brought the parrot home, her lovely twin daughters came home for the weekend from university.

Just as they got in the door, the bird spied them.

"Two more customer delights, delights, customer delights" it parroted.

The mother severely chastised the bird.

About two hours later, her husband came through the door.

Suddenly, the wisened, feathered one spoke up, "Now, there's a familiar face, familiar face, familiar face."

Pleasure in the job puts perfection in the work.

YOUR ATTITUDE WILL DETERMINE YOUR SUCCESS

(Gift from a wise Newfoundlander)

If you think you're beaten, you are,
If you think you dare not, you don't.
If you like to win, but think you can't,
It's almost certain you won't.

If you think you'll lose, you're lost,
For out in the world, you'll find,
Success begins with a person's will,
It's all in your state of mind.

If you think you're outclassed, you are,
For you've got to think high, to rise.
You've got to be sure of yourself before,
You can ever win a prize.

The battles of life don't always go
To the stronger or faster man,
But sooner or later the one who wins
Is the man WHO **THINKS** HE CAN.

WHIZ
Nflder: "First I got appendicitis and pneumonia. Then, I got erysipelas with hemachromatosis. After that I got poliomyelitis and finally ended up with neuritis. Following that they gave me hypodermics and inoculations."
Tronnie: "Boy, you've sure had a tough time of it."
Nfldr: "You betcha. Never thought I'd make it through that spelling test."

DISGUISE
How can normal people recognize Tronnies?
Easy.
No matter how they dress...
they still look like turkeys.

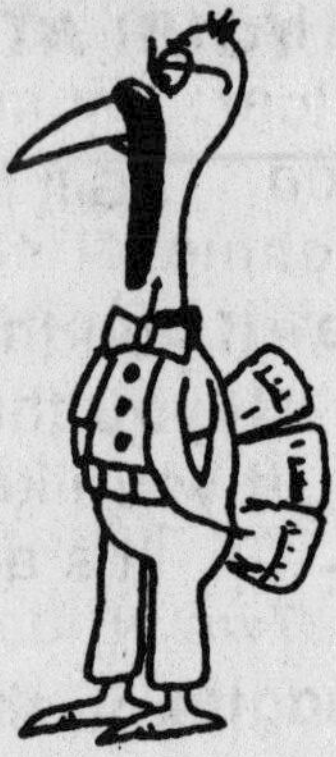

HOTEL HOAX
Why are garbage cans painted orange in Tronna?
So Tronnies will think they are eating out at Howard Johnson's.

What do you get when you cross a donkey with a Tronnie?
An ass that looks like a turkey.

Tronnies are famous for foot-in-the-mouth disease.

HE KNOWS
Why wasn't God born in Tronna?
He could find neither three wise men nor a virgin.

SUPER TUTORS
What was Newfoundland's humanitarian - oriented centennial project?
Grade five graduates were sent to teach in Tronnie high schools.

WHAT A LIE
Nflder: "Mom told me that fish is great brain food."
Tronnie: "I know. I eat it all the time."
Newf: "Looks like Mom lied."

FLICK TRICK

Two Nflders came out of a movie theatre. Judging by the looks on their faces it must have been a pretty poor flick. One turned to the other and said, "Paddy, isn't it wonderful grand how movies have advanced these past few years?"

"Whaddya mean b'y? asked the other.

"Well, first, there were silent pictures, then. there were talkies, and now this one stinks.

LOONEY LIMEY

Heard about the frustrated Englishman in Tronna who was seen biting a handful of Loonie Gold Coins, when they first came on the market.

A Newfoundlander standing nearby approached the poor, wretched limey and asked, "What are you doing biting those things?"

The Englishman, more than just a little upset, demanded, "Leave me alone, can't you see, I'm trying to get the chocolate out!"

WHAT YOU SEE IS WHAT YOU GET
To a pessimist, a bottle is half empty.
To an optimist, it's half full.

LONG AND SHORT OF IT

The Tronnie told the Nflder he'd saved up his money to buy a farm.
Nflder: "What's it look like?"
Tronnie: "Ten miles long and half an inch wide."
Newf: "Whaddya gonna raise on it?
Tronnie: "Spaghetti?"

FREEDOM OF SPEECH

A Tronnie was yapping away, as they are prone to do, patronizing the Newfoundlander. After four or five boring minutes of babbling, he said, "I believe in freedom of speech!" The Newf waiting to get a word in edgewise, allowed, "That's wonderful b'y. Yer a fine fella. Hand me yer phone 'til I calls the island."

Hear about the Tronnie who kept learning more and more about less and less until now he knows everything about nothing.

NAVIGATION

Don't wait for your ship to come in;
Swim out to it.

NOTHING TO CROW ABOUT

Hear about the rooster who was so lazy, he waited until all the others crowed, and then, just nodded his head.

SCRAM
Tronnie: "Newf, what steps would you take if you saw a dangerous lion on the loose?"
Newf: "Long ones, me son. Bloody big long ones."

COMMON SENSE

Tronnie: "Every time I drink a cup of tea, I get this stabbing pain in my right eye. Whaddya think I should do about it?"

Newf: "No problem, me son. Take the spoon out of yer cup first."

NO FOOLING
The Tronnie calls his new neighbour, recently arrived from Newfoundland.
"Is this Pat?"
"Yup, this is he."
"Doesn't sound like Pat."
"Listen, me son, I know who I am, It's definitely me."
"Can you lend me $10, Pat?"
"I'll ask him just as soon as he comes in. See ya."

Tronnie: "Newf, what makes you so hard-boiled?"
Nflder: "Because I've been in hot water so many times."

If you want to point out a concrete example... ask a Tronnie to remove his hat.

CUT UP
It's well known that those responsible for the Tronna education system have finally gotten the message and have started upgrading. In this regard, they have hired a goodly number of Newfoundland teachers.
One elderly fella in particular, quickly became a favourite in a high school class, due to his ability to bridge the generation gap.
On his fourth day, the class beauty, the pre-madonna, showed up late sporting a dazzling red Mohawk haircut and painted face. The wily Newf prof studied her for a moment or two and then to roars of great glee from the class, intoned, "You appear, my dear, to have had a very narrow escape."

Enthusiasm is contagious. The person who has it under control is usually welcome anywhere.

FAX
Did you know a facsimile message to Nova Scotia's capital is called A Halifax.

Tronnie: "Newf, d'ya think it's true that carrots are good for the eyesight?"

Newf: "Ever see a rabbit wearing glasses?"

Heard about the Tronnie who thought NO KIDDING was a birth control pill?

Then there was the Tronnie who thought MANUAL LABOUR was a Mexican.

Tronnies think A MUSHROOM is a place to neck?

What do the Argos and the Leafs have in common?
Neither can play hockey.

There's a new Tronnie doll on the market.
It talks all day and bad-mouths everybody.

Hear about the Tronnie who spent two days at Sears looking for a miscarriage?

Then, there was the bright Tronnie
who took a roll of toilet paper to a crap game.

Hear about the Tronnie who failed his I.Q. test?

Then there was the story of the defeat of the Commons member from Tronna. It was big news. A classic case of the bull throwing the politician.

DEAD RECKONING
It's not the way the wind blows,
It's the way you set your sails.

Hear about the Tronnie who cooked the chicken for two days because the cookbook said to cook one half hour to the pound and she weighs 110 pounds?

Tronnie to Nfld pilot: "How are we doing?"
Newf: "We're lost, but we're making excellent time."

BEHIND TIME

The Tronnie apartment dweller shouted below to his neighbour from Nfld, "If you don't stop playing that blasted accordion,

I'll go crazy."

"Guess it's too late," the Nflder shot back, "I stopped an hour ago."

A elderly Tronnie woman, visiting St. John's for the first time, saw a well-lit sign on the front of a multi-level building. It read: "The Smith Manufacturing Co."
"My Lord," the old dear exclaimed, "I've heard of Smiths all my life, but I never knew where they made them."

Tronnies are so dumb...
mind readers only charge them half price.

KNOWS NOSES

A young Tronnie said to his father, "Pop, there was a man here to see you today."

Dad: "Did he have a bill?"

Son: "No, Pop, just an ordinary nose like yours."

SWEET THING

Hear about the Nflder who had a Tronnie girl friend he called Vinegar Kitty?

She was such a sour puss.

FAIR TRADER

Two judges, one a Nflder, the other a Tronnie, were arrested for speeding. When they arrived in court, no other judge was available. So, they decided to try each other.

The Tronnie judge went up to the bench and said, "You are charged with exceeding the speed limit. How do you plead?"

"Guilty!" was the answer.

"You are hereby fined five dollars."

Then they changed places, and again the plea was "Guilty!"

"Hmm!" said the Nfld judge. "These cases are becoming far too common. This is the second case of this sort we've had this morning. I hereby fine you twenty-five dollars or ten days in jail.

Criticism plants fear and resentment.
It never shows love or affection.

The Tronnie was asked what she thought of Red China? She said, "It's alright, as long as it doesn't clash with the tablecloth."

Tronnie: "Why is the nose in the middle of your face?"
Nflder: Because it's the scenter."

ASTUTE

"And how did you find the bath salts, ma'am?" asked the pharmacist.

"Well, they taste very nice," said the Tronnie woman, " but I don't think they have the same effect as a real bath."

Tronnie: "When do the leaves begin to turn?"
Newf: "The night before exams."

SELF DEFENSE EXPERT

A Nflder was telling a friend about a trick he'd learned while studying jiu-jitsu.

"So, I grabbed his wrist like this - then I grabbed his arm like this - then I twisted like this - and before he knew what hit him - I was flat on my back."

THE GREEN SCIENTIST

A green little chemist, on a green little day,
Mixed some green little chemicals, in a green little bay,
The green little grasses, now tenderly wave,
O'er the green little chemist's,
Green little grave.

CYRANO'S REGRET

It does not breathe, it does not smell,
It does not feel, too very well.
I am disgusted with my nose.
The only thing it does, is blows.

WHADDA LINE

Tronnie: "What's that gurgling noise I hear?"
Nfld girl: "It's me, trying to swallow that line of yours."

HEALTH NOT WEALTH

A wealthy Newfoundlander's will was read. It said: "To my friend, Sam Wassisname, I leave my phone company stocks....to my faithful valet, James Watchimacallit, I leave my city real estate... and to my intellectual nephew, Alexander, who always argued that health is more important than wealth, I leave an assortment of gym equipment including jogging shoes and sweat socks.

Hear about the Nflder who got a bill from Tronna, that said, "This bill's a year old." He wrote back, "Happy Birthday!"

BUZZ OFF BART

"Aren't you putting your saddle on backwards, sir?" asked the cowboy.
Tronnie gay: " That's all you know about it, smarty pants. You don't even know which way I'm going."

LOGIC

The ferry from the mainland was approaching Port aux Basques when it slowed to a near crawl due to dense fog.

An inquisitive passenger from Tronna visiting the bridge inquired of the captain the cause of the delay.

"Like pea soup out there, can't see a hand in front of ya," was his reply.

"But I can see the stars overhead," the passenger exclaimed in a sharp tone.

"Yes," the captain boomed, "but unless the boilers bust, we ain't goin' that way."

Hear about the Tronnie who's going to give up working and live by his wits. Well, half a living is better than none.

THEY WENT THATAWAY

The scene is Marble Mountain, Steady Brook, Nfld.

Lady tourist from Tronna: "What a beautiful mountain! There must be a great many romantic stories connected with it."

Local: "Yep, two lovers went up that mountain and never came back here."

Tronnie: "My, my, what ever became of them?"

Local: "Went down the other side."

What's a pimple on a Tronnie's backside?
A brain tumour.

Smile...and give your face a holiday.

QUESTION ABLE
Tronnie Salesman: "Is your mother home today, sonny?"
Young Nflder: "Yessir."
Tronnie... after knocking a few times: "I thought you said she was home."
Newf: 'She is, but we don't live here."

YOUNG WIT

A Tronnie, who believed Newfoundlanders ate only fish and brewis, asked a young lad in Twillingate one day, "How long do Newfoundlanders live?"

The lad: "Heard just the other day, they had to shoot an old fella to start a graveyard.

LAND OF MILK AAAND FUNNY
A part of Eastern Ontario is known as cattle country...where the men are men and the sheep are nervous.

COPIES
Tronnies act the same...loud, noisy, insulting...

'cause they were all made at the same record company.

PLEASANTLY POLITE

A Tronnie, down on his luck in St. John's, read in the paper, news of a convention of pleasantly plump ladies from around the island. It was to be held the following day.

Next morning, he parked himself at the entrance to the hotel. He'd heard these girls were a soft touch. They were so kindhearted, they would give unstintingly and without question.

As a likely subject approached, he turned on his act.

"Lady," he begged, "please have mercy on me. I haven't eaten for four days."

"My word!" she gasped, "I certainly wish I had your will power."

Heard about the two Tronna gays... Gerald Fitzpatrick and Patrick Fitzgerald?

THE TRUTH AND NOTHING BUT

"What is your age?" the magistrate asked the Newfoundlander. "Remember," he cautioned, "You're under oath."

"Twenty-one years and some months," the lady from Nfld answered.

"How many months?"

"Two hundred and eight."

Tronnies never get lost.
People are always telling them where to go.

In a battle of wits...Tronnies fight unarmed.

TRONNIE IN ICE HOLE
How do you get a Tronnie in an ice hole?
First, you place peas in a chain around the hole,
Then, you wait 'til he comes out to take a pea.
And then, you kick him in the hole.

WILL MEN EVER LEARN?
I'm through with women, they cheat and they lie.
They'll prey on we males 'til the day we die.
They tease and torment us, and drive us to sin...
Hey! Look at that blond who just came in!

THE TRONNA COLLEGE CROWD

You can tell a freshman,
by his silly, eager look.
You can tell a sophomore,
'cause he carries one less book.
You can tell a junior,
by his dashing air and such.
You can tell a senior,
but b'y, you can't tell him much.

Tronnie: Imagine if money were no object
Newf: "Yes m'son. I'd definitely want none."

WHAT A DOG!
She ate a hotdog with relish, and rolled her eyes above.
She ate a half dozen more, and died of puppy love.

BELIEVE IT OR NOT

A Tronna college lecturer announced to the class that the world would probably end in about six billion years.

"How long did you say?" asked a terrified voice from the rear.

"Seven billion years,"

"Thank God," said the voice, "I thought for a moment there you said seven million."

ABSENT MINDED PROF

Tronnie Professor: "My dear, I hate to mention it, but the toast is terribly tough this morning,"
Wife: "Oh, darling, I hate to mention it, but that's the cork mat you're eating."

APPRECIATION PLUS

Curious Nfider: "Does your wife ever pay you any compliments?"
Nonchalant Tronnie: "Only in the winter."
Newf: "How so?"
"Well, when the fire gets low, she says, "Alexander...the grate!"

LOVE LUMPS

I took her to a concert, I took her to a show,
I took her almost everywhere,
a girl and boy could go.
I took her to super dances,
I took her out to tea,
And when all my bucks were gone, I saw
She'd been taking me.

RIGHT FOOT FORWARD

A NIfder treated his wife to a trip to Tronna's Roy Thompson Hall. After intermission the couple returned to their seats in the dark auditorium. The Newf asked the fella seated next to the aisle if someone had stepped on his foot while leaving before the break.

"Yes, YOU did," he responded, expecting an apology.

"Okay, honey," beckoned the downhomer to wifey, "this is our row."

ASTUTE MEDIC

A Newfy psychiatrist received a wild call about three o'clock in the morning. A former Tronnie patient, a kleptomaniac, shouted frantically,

"Doc, doc, you've gotta help me," he pleaded, "I've got that old urge to steal, again."

"Oh, for goodness sake," said the medic, "just take two ashtrays and call me in the morning."

There's one guaranteed way to keep mouthy Tronnies quiet for a few minutes. Put 'em in elevators. Watch 'em. Works everytime.

Hear about the university of Tronna ancient history student who thought that Phoenicians were famous for inventing BLINDS?

Hear about the Tronnie who's so stingy, when he finally lets go a breath of air...it's vacuum?"

Hear about the Nflder who nicknamed his new Tronnie girlfriend 'Appendix' because it took so much to take her out.

BELIEVE IT OR NOT

A Tronna college lecturer announced to the class that the world would probably end in about six billion years.

"How long did you say?" asked a terrified voice from the rear.

"Seven billion years,"

"Thank God," said the voice, "I thought for a moment there you said seven million."

ABSENT MINDED PROF

Tronnie Professor: "My dear, I hate to mention it, but the toast is terribly tough this morning,"
Wife: "Oh, darling, I hate to mention it, but that's the cork mat you're eating."

Tronnie guy: "What would I have to give you for just one little kiss?"
Nfld gal: "Chloroform."

Tronnie: I can't seem to get along with her. All she does is ignore me."
Newf: "Ignore You?"
Tronnie: Yeah - and if there's anything I hate, it's IGNORANCE."

PIGEON TALK

Not too long ago the weather office in St. John's received a phone call from a rather talkative type who said he was from Tronna and had come to retire on the island. He continued as to how he raised and raced pigeons, as a pastime. He went on to inquire about wind-flow patterns, cloud conditions and other technical matters.

The Nflder who answered the call explained the current meteorological status in great detail. The Tronnie apparently didn't understand the info and asked to have it repeated.

"Wearily," the Newf asked, "Please, let me talk to the pigeon!"

SOME STUNNED

A lady from Newfoundland who lived in Tronna for a few years applied for job in sales at a fabric shop. She was given a test to determine her knowledge of calculations, measurments and the like.

When it was over, the owner was astonished. She'd answered all the questions correctly. He immediately offered her a job.

"You wouldn't believe," he said with a deep sigh, "how many get eight or more wrong on this test."

"Oh, yes I would," she responded, "They've been waiting on me for years."

Most Tronnie kids are the kinda kids their parents don't want them to play with.

NO SALE

A Tronnie was promoted to export manager for a Newfoundland company. He worked out of the big smoke office. He sent a communique to his boss on the island endeavouring to sell him on a necessary trip to Cuba via cruise ship.

"This is the most efficient means of travel," he explained, "The package includes meals, transportation and lodging."

A return fax message read: "NO SAIL."

Tronnie: "There goes a sensible girl."

Nflder: "Yeah, *she wouldn't go out with me either."*

Hear about the Tronnie they call Miner?

She makes the most of her natural resources.

NEVER TAKE NO

The Nflder and his Tronnie wife arrived home quite late after a party. As the wife was getting ready for bed the Newf hurried into the kitchen and returned with a glass of water and two aspirin. After he handed the pills to his spouse, she asked, "What's this?"

"Aspirin," he said.

"But I don't have a headache," she replied sternly.

"Aha!" boomed the husband gleefully.

"Gotcha!"

COMMON SENSE

Tronnie Cop: "Do you know who I am?"
Newf: " Hey Mikey.
We got a policeman here who's not sure who he is."

MISTAKEN IDENTITY

The newly married Tronnie woman was testifying in court. "This man broke into my house at 3 o'clock in the morning."
"And did he get anything?" asked the lawyer.
"Yes," she replied. "I thought it was my husband coming home from night shift."

COMING OR GOING?

The Tronnie was at the bar and about three sheets in the wind. The bartender realized the man was too drunk already, and when the customer ordered another drink the barkeep refused to serve him. The drunk was indignant and said, "I'll prove to you that I'm not drunk and still in command of all my senses. D'you see that cat coming in the room? Well, it's only got one eye." The bartender said, "No more drinking for you— that cat's not coming in, it's going out!

A REAL PILL

Tronnie Patient: "Doctor, I'd like something to make me smarter."
Doctor: "Take these pills and come back to see me next week."
Tronnie Patient (next week): "Doc, I don't think I'm any smarter."
Doctor: "Take these pills and come back to see me next week."
Tronnie Patient (next week): "Doc, I don't think I've gotten any smarter yet. Are you sure these pills aren't candy?"
Doctor: "Now you're getting smarter."

SEND A COPY TO A FRIEND......

We'll forward a copy of **THE TRONNA ROAST #1** to anyone for you!

Here's all you do. . .Send complete Name and Address along with a certified cheque or money order for $6.50 for each copy you wish mailed. We'll forward it with your compliments and a message, if you wish.

Please use the following form. If you have more than one order, enclose an extra sheet of paper with all the necessary information, using the same format as contained herein.

Please send a copy of **TRONNA ROAST #1** to....

Name ______________________________

Address ______________________________

City ____________________ Province ____________

Postal Code ________________

Send your orders to: **Tronna Roast #1**
c/o Upalong Enterprises
Box 429
Port Sydney, Ont.
P0B 1L0

CONFUSIN' AIN'T IT?

"Look before you leap" or "He who hesitates is lost."
"Two heads are better than one" or "Too many cooks spoil the broth."
"Absence makes the heart grow fonder" or "Out of sight, out of mind."
"You can't teach an old dog new tricks" or "A man is never too old to learn."
"All things come to him who waits" or "Time and tide wait for no man."
"Fine feathers make fine birds" or "Don't judge a book by its cover."
"Two's company, three's a crowd" or "The more the merrier."

"Bottoms Up, You All!"